Harvest Waiting

Donald Moorman

PUBLISHING HOUSE
3558 SOUTH JEFFERSON AVENUE
SAINT LOUIS, MISSOURI 63118-3968

Copyright ©1993 Concordia Publishing House
3558 South Jefferson Avenue, St. Louis, MO 63118-3968
Manufactured in the United States of America

Library of Congress Cataloging-in-Publication Data

Moorman, Donald. 1943-
Harvest waiting / Donald Moorman.
p. cm.
Includes bibliographical references and index.
ISBN 0-570-09936-6 : $9.95
1. Church work with immigrants--United States. 2. Church work
with refugees--United States. 3. United States--Church history.
4. United States--Church history--20th century.   I. Title.
BV639.I4M66 1993
261.8'348'00973--dc20   93-21088
                                                              CIP

1 2 3 4 5 6 7 8 9 10   02 01 00 99 98 97 96 95 94 93

DEDICATION

This book is dedicated to all of those who, from my childhood, have helped me move to the edge of my own culture so that I could appreciate the beauty of other cultures. Some have pushed me and others have led me, but all have helped accomplish the Lord's will in my life. I am thankful to God for all of the pain, self-discovery and new insights which led to this book!

CONTENTS

INTRODUCTION

Growing up in rural southern Indiana, I was surrounded by the realities of farming. Four of these apply to the present opportunities and challenges the church faces in multi-cultural America. The first and most basic reality of farming is that without water there are no crops. The rain which God sends from heaven allows the miracle of germination, growth, maturity and harvest to happen. Second, there are certain basic principles a farmer must understand and use regardless of what kind of farming he does. Every farmer has to know how to plow, fertilize, plant, cultivate, harvest and sell whatever crop he decides to grow. Third, each crop takes specialized knowledge and specialized machinery. A farmer must have certain specialized knowledge of each crop he grows. Farming corn is different from farming alfalfa, which is different from farming wheat, and so on. Also, a farmer must have access to specialized harvesting machines for each of his crops. He cannot harvest wheat with the best corn picker, and he cannot harvest corn with the most sophisticated hay baler. Fourth, the successful farmer must constantly update his equipment. The threshing machine was great in its time, but its time has long since passed. No modern farmer could get the best from his land by using outdated machinery.

In John 4:35, Jesus says, "Open your eyes and look at the fields! They are ripe for harvest." In the United States today there are many ethnic communities which can properly be seen as fields "ripe for harvest." If we are to reap those harvests we must approach them with the daily prayer that God would rain down blessings on our efforts. We are doing God's work, and it is only through His grace that we can reap the harvest-laden fields which surround us. This is the proper spiritual preparation for the task before us.

We should also prepare ourselves intellectually for the harvest. We should expand our knowledge so that we can understand the best ways to reap this unique harvest the Lord has put before us. We must have an understanding of our nation's long history of immigrants and of refugees. This understanding will help us see the similarities between the current immigrants and refugees and those who arrived earlier. Some lessons of the past will serve us well for the future. They will also help us appreciate the differences. Some of today's realities are absolutely unique. The old lessons, in some cases, will be of little help. In those instances, we need to be open to learn new ways of adapting to new situatuations.

We must also develop a basic sociological and philosphical framework which will give shape to our ministry, regardless of which culture we are addressing. There are several questions we must ask ourselves as we reach out to other cultural groups with the message of salvation. It is not enough to say simply that we intend to proclaim the Gospel. Of course that is our central purpose, but the question is: How do we proclaim the Gospel of Christ effectively in different cultures? Of course we recognize that it is the Holy Spirit who works the miracle of faith in the hearts of people, but the question is: Which approaches to ministry allow Him the best opportuntity to work that miracle in people whose culture is different from ours? No doubt we will want to maintain the biblical heart of our faith as we transfer it to a new culture, but the question is: Which parts of our identity as a church are doctrinally based and therefore mandatory for any group which bears our name, and which parts are based on culture and therefore must be transformed as our church takes root in a new culture?

This book is designed to help the church answer those basic questions. I had two goals as I prepared the following material. First, I tried to present the material in a way that those who are on the front lines of cross-cultural ministry will find easy to read and understand. It is intended as a usable tool in the harvest, not as a scholarly treatise. Second, I have tried to present an accurate picture of the challenges before us and the possible ways of responding to those challenges. Cross-cultural ministry presents us with many complexities and subtleties which we need to understand before we can respond effectively to the opportunities the Lord has given us. In addressing these complexities and subtleties, I have tried to present material that is easy to understand without being simplistic. For this reason, prayer and research went hand in hand as I prepared this material.

Together with this primer, Concordia Publishing House is publishing a series of small books, each dealing with a particular nationality or ethnic group. Each book has been designed to provide the information needed by the local congregation or individual to reach out with the Gospel to the "stranger" in their midst. My purpose is to present the basic principles which are valid in all the fields into which our Lord sends us.

This book provides the basic theoretical background necessary for anyone interested in ministry with people of a different culture. It will also be useful in convincing the skeptic that culturally sensitive ministry in the midst of today's ethnic diversity is historically, sociologically, and theologically sound. The questions at the end of each chapter are designed for personal reflection and group discussion. The appendices at the end of this book are designed to help a congregation devise a workable plan for moving, step by step, into fruitful ministry with people from another culture.

My prayer is that God will use the insights in this book to motivate and equip the Christian Church to reach out to the many new people groups in the United States with the saving power of the Gospel.

1
IMMIGRANTS AND REFUGEES— A HISTORICAL SKETCH

T he United States is a nation of immigrants and refugees from all over the world. Immigrants came in order to find a better life for themselves and their children. Life in their country of origin was difficult and offered few opportunities for the future, and so they came seeking "greener pastures" in the United States. Until the twentieth century, most who came to the United States entered as immigrants. Refugees came because they faced religious, racial or political persecution. It was no longer feasible for them to continue life in their country of origin, for life there meant danger, suffering and, quite possibly, death. Most people who have come to the United States as refugees have come during the twentieth century, though refugees have been fleeing to the United States from the beginning of its history.

LEVELS OF ACCEPTANCE

The United States has always been very conscious of different kinds of immigrants and refugees. The most accepted were white and Protestant. White Catholics in general experienced a certain amount of resistance and even some outright hostility before they were accepted. Jewish people likewise had to overcome hostility to their presence in the United States. Non-whites, however, have always had the most difficulty being accepted and have always endured the greatest amount of hostility of any of the immigrants and refugees. Black Africans were imported as slaves and were denied basic human rights for nearly 250 years. Asians, being both non-white and non-Christian, have, historically, borne the brunt of a double dose of hostility.

These different levels of acceptance point out that Americans have not been as open to the world and all of its peoples as popular imagination has believed. "For 162 years, the Naturalization Law, while allowing various European or 'white' ethnic groups to enter the United States and acquire citizenship, specifically denied citizenship to other groups on a racial basis. While suffrage was extended to white men, it was withheld from men of color. Thus, what actually developed historically in American society was a pattern of citizenship and suffrage which drew a very sharp distinction between 'ethnicity' and 'race.'"[1] Even though the Immigration Act of 1965 removed the racial bias from the official immigration policy of the United States, the old attitude that white people make the best and most reliable Americans has persisted. As we shall see, this is an attitude rooted deeply in the American soul.

ECONOMICS AND ACCEPTANCE OF IMMIGRANTS

Another factor which influenced the level of acceptance of newcomers to the United States was the state of the economy when the various groups arrived. During those times when the economy in the United States was expanding and there was a shortage of workers, most immigrants were welcomed and some even recruited. During the various depressions and recessions the nation has experienced, immigrants were unwelcome, for the resident population did not want newcomers competing with them in a shrinking economy.

THE TIME DIFFERENCE IN ARRIVAL
OF WHITES AND NON-WHITES

Another important factor in the immigrant and refugee picture is when they arrived. The vast majority of white immigrants and refugees arrived before 1930. The vast majority of non-white immigrants and refugees came after 1880 with the floodgates really opening only after the Immigration Act of 1965. The major exception to this pattern was, of course, Black Africans, who were imported as slaves as early as the 1600s. By the time other non-white groups began arriving in significant numbers, blacks had already been in the United States for over 200 years, first as slaves and then as an oppressed underclass. Another exception were the many tribes of Native Americans, most of which were exterminated as Europeans took over the land. The United States added to the shame of extermination by denying citizenship to Native Americans until 1924.

HISTORICAL SKETCHES OF IMMIGRANT AND REFUGEE GROUPS

To get the flavor of the immigrants and refugees who have made the United States what it is today, we will look at several groups of immigrants and refugees who make up the mosaic of the United States. Perhaps we can begin to appreciate our current groups of immigrants and refugees by looking back at earlier groups.

THE FIRST EUROPEANS

The first Europeans to arrive in the area that would become the United States were a curious blend of adventurers anxious to explore the New World, businessmen and entrepreneurs who came to make their fortunes and return to Europe as wealthy men, and religious dissidents who came so they could practice religious beliefs which were persecuted in Europe. In a way, these religious dissidents were the first refugees to come to the United States.

THE ENGLISH

In the colonial period the major immigrant group was the English. The first great English immigration was tied to a calamitous time in England. From 1603 to 1688, England was ruled by a series of three kings from the house of Stuart who sought to crush the power of the Parliament and rule by "divine right." This led to endless political strife. Depending on who was dominant in this strife at any given time, certain groups in English society either prospered or were persecuted.

No social or economic group enjoyed any guarantees of stability. Even the wealthy landowners often lived on borrowed money and teetered on the brink of bankruptcy. For the poor—and they made up the bulk of the population—life was "nasty, brutish, and short"[2] and the rigid class barriers in the society made upward mobility impossible.

The period also suffered under the pressures of overpopulation, unemployment and three major depressions. Adding to the suffering and terror of the times were recurrent outbreaks of bubonic plague. In 1625, "5,205 Londoners and another 4,000 in the suburbs of Westminster and Stepney died in a single week."[3]

So, from the wealthy on down to the poverty stricken, the English population had reason to look for some opportunity to make a new beginning. The colonies beckoned as a peaceful place where new opportunties were available and upward mobility was possible. Between 1620 and 1642 "eighty thousand English (close to two percent of the population)"[4] left the country, the majority heading for the colonies. Most traveled in the crowded holds of cargo ships where they suffered hunger, disease, and vermin infestation. At times things were so bad that those who died were cannibalized so that others could survive the trip.

Many began life in the colonies as indentured servants who had to endure years of near slavery before they could even begin to pursue their dreams. They brought with them not only their dreams for a better life but also a cultural heritage which included the social, political and legal structures which still nourish the United States today.

THE GERMANS

The Germans were another group which began arriving in the United States during colonial times. At first they trickled in individually and in small groups. In the early and mid 1600s they, along with the Dutch, settled in New Amsterdam (now New York) and prospered. "By 1745, there were an estimated 45,000 Germans in Pennsylvania,"[5] with the majority living in the Philadelphia area. At the time of the American Revolution there were approximately 300,000 people of German descent in the Colonies which represented about 10 percent of the total population.[6] They were, at the time, the largest and most conspicuous non-English group in the United States. Most of the German immigrants were farmers, and these farmers developed, among other things, a covered wagon, the Conestoga wagon, which would later play a major role in the westward expansion of the population.

The great German immigration occurred in the 1840s and 1850s. The potato blight, which would soon devastate Ireland, struck Germany also and was the motivation for thousands of farmers to make their way to the United States with their families. But there were more than simple farmers among the German immigrants. From the 1820s on, many highly educated Germans who were politically and socially liberal were migrating to the United States. Their liberalism put them at odds with the conservative and often repressive German government, and rather than fight what seemed to be a losing battle, they left for the United States. Still others, such as the Saxons under the leadership of Martin Stephan, came in order to practice their particular brand of theological orthodoxy. The growing German communities in the United States even contained numbers of German Jews whose affinity for things German made them prefer German enclaves over Jewish.

More than 50,000 Germans arrived in 1846 and more than 200,000 arrived in 1854.[7] The majority of these were farmers and settled mainly in the upper Mississippi and Ohio valleys. The main urban centers of the German immigrants were St. Louis, Milwaukee, and Cincinnati. One exception to this general trend of midwestern settlement was Texas. Many Germans were attracted to Texas by the low price of land, and by 1857, Texas had some thirty-five thousand German settlers.

By 1900, there were about 8,000,000 people in the United States who were born in Germany or of German descent. They lived in tightly knit communities, spoke German, developed German social and religious organizations and produced many German language newspapers. Gradually they moved into most major professions and trades and by 1972 "only 8 percent of German males were still farmers or farm laborers."[8] While they have diversified professionally, they have remained a strong ethnic presence in the midwestern section of the country.

THE AFRICANS

Black Africans also appeared in the United States during the colonial period. They, unique among ethnic groups in the United States, were neither immigrants nor refugees, but were brought here against their will to serve as slaves. The first African slaves were brought here in 1619. By the 1640s, black African slaves were already an established part of the colonial economy, and by 1661, a law was passed which established slavery as an institution. That law declared that children of slaves were automatically slaves. These slaves received no constitutional protection and were not accorded the privileges of citizenship. There was also a small number of free Blacks in the colonies. One free Black, Crispus Attucks, died on March 5, 1770, while leading the Boston Massacre, an attack on British soldiers who were stationed at the Boston Custom House. This made him one of the first casualties of the Revolution.

The country's appetite for slaves grew quickly. In 1754, there were 298,000 slaves in the colonies. "In 1790 the first United States census would count 697,681"[9] and by 1800, Black slaves accounted for 20 percent of the country's population. Their journey to the United States was nightmarish. Africans were crammed into the holds of cargo ships where they "had to wallow in pools of their own excrement, urine, vomit and bloody mucus from ever-present dysentery."[10] It is little wonder that in many cases nearly a quarter of the Africans died on their journey to slavery.

In the 1700s, slaves learned and practiced many trades for the profit of their masters and even—occasionally—for their own profit. By the 1800s, however, almost all slaves were confined to the hard life of plantation field work. By law they were barred from even rudimentary education. White Christians made little efforts to win Blacks to Christianity for fear that certain teachings of the church might encourage them to seek freedom. There were occasional slave uprisings, such as the one in 1831 in Virginia led by Nat Turner, but the institution of slavery functioned so efficiently that there was surprisingly little violence committed by the slaves.

The Emancipation Proclamation of 1863 extended freedom to all slaves. Little help, however, was given to the former slaves as they began their lives as free citizens. The half million free Blacks were relatively unaffected by Emancipation. During the Civil War, about 10 percent of the Union Army troops were Black and "twenty-one blacks won the Congressional Medal of Honor."[11]

Following the Civil War, life didn't change much for most Blacks. By 1877, the Reconstructionists had, by and large, abandoned their efforts to reshape southern society and the Blacks were left to fend for themselves. In the south, most continued to work the land, in many cases living on the same plantations which had once held them as slaves. Their day-to-day situation differed little from their life before Emancipation. Gangs of terrorists such as the Ku Klux Klan used whatever means they deemed necessary to keep Blacks "in their place." In the north most Blacks were employed as domestic servants, and though certain aspects of their lives were easier than those of their counterparts in the south, they still functioned as an oppressed underclass largely ignored by the rest of society. Many of the freed slaves did not understand how to function in a free society and so were easy prey for those who sought to take advantage of them. Gradually, however, they gained social sophistication, took advantage of educational opportunities and developed social, legal and political organizations which helped them to appropriate the privileges of freedom.

From the beginning of Black advancement two voices were heard from the black community, one accomodating and one confrontational. Chief among those seeking advancement through accomodation was Booker T. Washington. Brought to national prominence by his tireless devotion to the development of Tuskegee Institute in Alabama, Washington sought a progress for Blacks which stressed a combination of Black self-reliance and cooperation on the part of the white community. He worked for economic opportunities for blacks but advocated what seemed to be a "separate but equal" philosophy in the arena of social relationships. White society gave him applause and honors but almost no cooperation.

An early voice of confrontation was the firey eloquence of Frederick Douglass. A veteran of the abolitionist movement, he saw the need for Blacks to demand their birthright as free Americans, not beg for it. W. E. B. DuBois, who, along with other prominant Blacks, founded the NAACP in 1909, also believed in confrontation—though the NAACP carried out its confrontations mainly in courtrooms. Marcus Garvey, also a confrontationalist, was, perhaps, the first to champion Black power and Black pride.

Immigrating to the United States from the West Indies in 1916, he founded a newspaper, the *Negro World*, whose battle cry was "Up, you mighty race! You can accomplish what you will."[12] Ultimately, however, he became so disillusioned with the United States that he championed a back-to-Africa movement. His activities in connection with that movement landed him in jail. "In 1927 he was pardoned and deported to Jamaica; he died in London in 1940."[13] The tensions between those who would accomodate and those who would confront continue to divide the Black community today.

For the first twenty years after Emancipation, the vast majority of Blacks stayed in the south, but in the 1880s and 1890s they began a major migration to the urban Northeast and Midwest. Between 1920 and 1930, more than 750,000 Blacks moved north.[14] The boll weevil, which severely disrupted southern agriculture, combined with a dramatic upswing in job opportunities in the factories of the Midwest and Northeast, fueled this migration. Most unions were antagonistic toward Blacks, and the factory jobs they did get were the dirtiest, the most dangerous, the most back-breaking and had the least possibilities of advancement, but at least they were jobs.

During the Depression, the migration slowed; by the 1940s, it had accelerated again with more than 1 million moving north during the 1940s. Between 1940 and 1970 more than 4 million Blacks migrated north, making this migration one of the greatest population movements in world history.[15] The migration carried Blacks from the rural south to the urban north. In essence, they had to start all over again in a completely new and sometimes frightening environment. Though they had been in the United States for 300 years, it was almost as though they had just arrived from some underdeveloped nation halfway around the world. They had to learn to adapt to a whole new environment.

In spite of some failures they not only adapted to their new situation but summoned the courage and skills to demand and receive their birthright as free people equal to all others. The Civil Rights Movement which gained national stature in the late 1950s is a testimony to the courage and abilities of Blacks. The landmark Civil Rights Act of 1964 was a direct result of that movement. The Civil Rights Act not only meant that it was okay to be Black but also that it was okay to be Hispanic or Asian. It created the context in which the cultural pluralism of the late twentieth century could develop. Thomas Sowell, commenting on Black history, says the following: "The race as a whole has moved from a position of utter destitution—in money, knowledge, and rights—to a place alongside other groups emerging in the great struggles of life. None have had to come from so far back to join their fellow Americans."[16]

One final note about a small group of Blacks who were a part of the migration to the Northeast but who came from the West Indies and not the rural southern United States. These, too, were the descendants of slaves, slaves who had received their freedom on August 1, 1838. Though the West Indian slaves and the slaves in the United States shared a heritage of physical brutality, there were important historical differences between them. While the West Indian slaves were expected to be self-reliant and to develop a subsistence economy which would provide for their necessities of life, the North American slaves were expected to rely on the plantation storehouse for all provisions and, in most cases, were forbidden to develop any kind of subsistence economy. West Indian Blacks began freedom with a long tradition of self-reliance and economic experience. North American Blacks began freedom out of a background which punished self-reliance and afforded no economic experience. These differences seem to have given a significant advantage to the West Indian Blacks in comparison to the North American Blacks as both groups grappled with the responsibilities and challenges of freedom after their emancipation.

Beginning in the first decade of the twentieth century there was a steady stream of West Indian Blacks immigrating to the United States, and they have fared quite well in their new country. In the United States, "West Indians have been about 1 percent of the black population but have been disproportionately overrepresented among black professionals, businessmen, and public figures."[17] Shirley Chisholm, Malcom X, Sidney Poitier and Harry Belafonte are just a few of the many Blacks of West Indian heritage who have achieved prominence. This fact has, at times, caused severe strains between Blacks with an American slave heritage and Blacks with a West Indian slave heritage.

THE JEWS

Jewish immigration was unique in that Jewish people came from many different countries but still had identity as an ethnic group because of their religion. Throughout history, the Jews of western and eastern Europe lived an uncertain existence. At times they were tolerated and their skills valued. At other times they were persecuted because of their religion, and representatives of Christianity tried to convert them by force. Sometimes they were driven out of a country simply because they were Jews. Because of these historical realities the Jewish people maintained their ethnic identity regardless of what country they were in, for they could never be sure how long it would be before they would be driven out. Because of their long history of both persecution and tolerance, it is hard to know whether they should be classed as immigrants or refugees. "Immigrant" probably applies to some groups and "refugee" to others. In this country, Jewish people found a greater degree of freedom than in most other places.

The first Jewish people to arrive in the colonies were descendants of the Sephardic Jews of Spain and Portugal. An interesting historical note: Spanish Jews, after a long period of toleration, were suddenly driven out of the country in 1492, the same year Columbus arrived in the Americas which would one day welcome them. These first Jewish immigrants arrived in 1654 and settled in New Amsterdam. There were twenty-three of them; they had come from a successful Jewish settlement in Brazil. In 1695, they established their first synagogue, located in New York City. German Jews also arrived during the colonial period. Unlike other Jews who formed their own communities, the German Jews often became a part of existing non-Jewish German communities. Their numbers were quite small at first. In 1776, there were only about 3,000 Jews living in the colonies; by 1850, the American Jewish population was still only about 30,000.[18]

It was not until the 1880s that great numbers of Jewish people began arriving in the United States. This huge new immigration came from Eastern Europe, with the vast majority from Russia. They came to escape crushing persecution which time after time had ravaged their communities and robbed them of their wealth. Many of them might properly be called refugees. Between

1880 and 1900, half a million Eastern European Jews came to the United States, and from 1900 to 1914, another million and a half arrived. The majority were so poor when they arrived that they stayed in New York City, many within walking distance of their point of arrival. Some, however, moved west, and soon there was a sizable Eastern European Jewish community in Chicago. Other Northeastern cities had small Eastern European Jewish communities. These Jews formed closely knit communities and did not often venture beyond them. The German Jews, who had prospered in the United States, tended to look down on these newly arrived Jews and tried to avoid associating with them.

The arrival of this large number of Jews was met with a growing anti-Semitism among the non-Jewish sectors of the population, and soon all Jews were victimized by harsh racist attitudes and policies. Some hated the Jews because they were not Christians. They held these new Jewish immigrants responsible for the death of Christ. Others looked down on the Jews as dirty, ignorant and unable to adapt to the American way of life. Still others feared that the Jews would never form any real loyalty to the United States. This was because, according to anti-semitic fears, the Jews were secretly plotting to rule the world.

Most of the Eastern European Jews worked as day laborers, skilled craftsmen, pushcart peddlers and laborers in the clothing industry. The Jewish community put a high value on education, and this helped them gradually expand their job opportunities and family wealth in the United States. The Jewish people of today are mainly concentrated in the Northeast and the West Coast, with the vast majority still in the Northeast.

THE CHINESE

There are reports of Chinese in the United States as early as 1571, but the American Immigration Commission records 1820 as the year the first Chinese entered the United States. Between 1820 and 1840, only ten Chinese arrived. One reason was that Chinese law mandated severe punishment for anyone caught trying to leave the country. Even after the legal barriers were removed, the upper classes in Chinese society exerted whatever social pressure they could to prevent emigration.

It was not until the early 1850s that significant numbers of Chinese began coming to the United States. There had been recurrent political unrest in Kwantung and Fukin provinces since the Manchu conquest of that area in 1644. Overpopulation in certain areas of China began to cause problems after 1800. In 1849, a terrible flood killed some 10,000, and in 1851, the Taiping Revolution began—which lasted fourteen years and caused in excess of 30,000,000 casualties.[19] Mercenary forces from the United States, Britain and France were also roaming the land in the 1800s, causing much death and destruction. From time to time there were violent uprisings against all foreigners. All of these factors combined to drive hundreds of thousands from their ancestral villages, and many of these uprooted people made their way to Hong Kong, Macao, and Canton. They hoped to find work, get help from family, or go abroad to earn money so they could return to their families and begin life again as wealthy men. In 1848, gold was discovered in California, and this news spread rapidly among the impoverished, uprooted Chinese whose situation was rapidly deteriorating. California gold loomed as the solution to all their problems.

Soon Chinese immigrants were flocking to the gold mining areas of California. They didn't intend to settle permanently in the United States; their goal was to accumulate three hundred ounces of gold—the amount of gold necessary to reestablish their lives in China—and return home. For this reason, the Chinese immigrants were overwhelmingly young males. Few brought their families with them. However, many never achieved their goal, so that what began as a temporary stay became permanent. By 1850, there were 4,000 Chinese in California. That same year, the first anti-Chinese legislation was passed: the Foreign Miners License Tax Law. This legislation forced Chinese gold miners to pay special taxes. Between 1850 and 1860, additional taxes were imposed on Chinese miners, and two special taxes were levied on shipmasters who brought Chinese to California.

While there were many Chinese gold miners, they never dominated the mining areas. By the end of the 1850s, they made up only about 25% of the miners in California. Many chose not to compete with whites for mining claims. They simply worked mines which had been abandoned as unprofitable by whites. They paid their taxes and tried to avoid confrontation, but they were still the targets of repeated harassment and violence. From 1854 until 1874, they lost most of their legal protection. During that period a law was in force in California which prevented "Chinese from testifying in court against white men—in effect, declaring open season on the Chinese, who had no legal recourse when robbed, vandalized or assaulted."[20] In spite of all this, the Chinese miners accounted for a quarter of the gold brought out of the California mines.

In 1860, there were 34,933 Chinese in the United States. By this time there were significant numbers of Chinese fishermen working the coastal California waters. "In 1860, Chinese fishermen were taxed. In addition, restrictive legislation regulated the size of the small-mesh fishing nets that they traditionally used. Chinese were forced into a limited market that would not be competitive with the rest of the industry."[21] As the gold mines of California played out, the Chinese moved to the mines of Oregon, Idaho, Montana, Nevada and Wyoming. Wherever they went they faced hostility and violence. By the 1860s, they were moving out of mining and into many other kinds of manual labor.[22]

The story of the construction of the Central Pacific Railroad is the story of the hard work and tenacity of Chinese immigrants. At the beginning, the work crews were predominantly white but soon almost all the whites quit because of the hardships involved. In response to this situation, Charles Crocker came up with the idea of recruiting Chinese to work on the project. By 1864, there were 4,000 Chinese workers on the railroad, compared to 1,000 white workers and at the peak of the project, in 1867, there were 10,000. Beginning in Sacramento, the Chinese crews worked under tremendously harsh conditions as they laid the tracks up the western slopes of the Sierras, across the rugged mountains and down the eastern side. All told, they built 1,600 miles of track. By comparison, the mostly Irish crews coming west moved across much gentler terrain and yet completed only 800 miles of track. In 1869, when the Transcontinental Railroad was completed, the eastern and western United States were joined. The railroad became a vital social and commercial link fostering the unity of the country. In 1870, 600 Chinese who were veterans of the Central Pacific

Railroad project helped build the Alabama and Chattanooga Railroad, and 250 helped build the Houston and Texas Railroad.

By 1870, there were over 64,000 Chinese in the United States. Most were concentrated along the west coast. Several hundred, however, were recruited to work on plantations in Mississippi, Georgia and Arkansas. In the 1870s, Chinese immigration continued to increase dramatically. By 1880, the Chinese population had increased to 105,465. Anti-Chinese activity also continued to increase. In 1871, Chinese quartz miners were expelled from Sutter's Creek. In 1872, California passed legislation which prohibited Chinese from owning real estate or obtaining a business license. They were the object of almost universal scorn and were denounced as the lowest form of humanity."[23] "They were considered incapable of being assimilated, culturally or biologically. They were feared as competitors whose hard work and longer hours for cheap pay would drive down the standard of living of American labor."[24] "Only the hardest, dirtiest, most menial jobs were open to them."[25] "In July of 1877, three days of anti-Chinese rioting rocked San Francisco,"[26] and a year later the city denied police protection to its Chinatown. In San Francisco, Chinese were not permitted to enter the municipal hospital, they were prohibited from voting, and their children were forced to attend segregated schools. In 1880, an angry mob drove all the Chinese out of Denver, Colorado, and burned their homes and businesses.

All of this anti-Chinese activity finally culminated in the passage of the Chinese Exclusion Act in 1882 which banned the entry of all skilled and unskilled Chinese laborers for ten years. "With the passage of this act the Chinese became the first and only nationality to be barred by name."[27] Certain Chinese professionals were still permitted to immigrate but Chinese immigration was reduced to a trickle. When the Act expired it was renewed for another ten years. One result of the Act was that it perpetuated the imbalance between males and females in the Chinese communities in the United States. There were no provisions to bring family members to the United States, so families were permanently separated. "By 1890, there were about twenty-seven Chinese men for every Chinese woman."[28] This meant that the Chinese communities produced few children. In most immigrant communities it was the children, who were enrolled in the public school, who brought the American culture and the English language back to the parents and the ethnic communities. This did not happen to any significant degree in the largely childless Chinese community and led to further isolation.

The Chinese Exclusion Act effectively stopped the dramatic increase of the Chinese population, but it didn't stop anti-Chinese activity. In 1885, while working as strikebreakers in a Rock Springs, Wyoming, coal mine, a group of Chinese was driven out of town by a mob of whites who burned their homes and murdered 28 of them.[29] In 1886, Eureka, California, Seattle and Tacoma, Washington, and Oregon City and Albina, Oregon, drove out their Chinese populations. Rioting miners of Douglas Island, Alaska, forced 100 Chinese to board small ships and set them adrift at sea. In 1902, Boston police illegally imprisoned and brutalized 234 Chinese, but no officer was ever disciplined for these actions. At the St. Louis World's Fair of 1904, the Chinese exhibitors, who had come at the invitation of the fair organizers, were treated like criminals and kept in virtual imprisonment.

In 1924, the Oriental Exclusion Act became law and banned the Chinese, as well as all other Asians, from immigrating to this country. In 1943, primarily because China was a World War II ally, the Chinese Exclusion Act was repealed. The McCarran-Walter Immigration Act of 1952 reaffirmed the position that the United States wanted to keep a tight control on all Asian immigration. In the years following 1949, the year when the Communists came to power in China, significant numbers of Chinese, over and above their normal immigration quota, were allowed entry into the United States as refugees. Finally, in 1965, with the passage of the Immigration Act of 1965 the door reopened for significant Chinese immigration. "The Chinese population almost doubled—from 237,000 to 435,000—in the decade of the 1960s,"[30] and by 1990 the Chinese population in the United States had swelled to 1,645,472.

With the passage of time and the gradual relaxation of the immigration laws regarding Asians, the imbalance between men and women was reduced, normal family life became more common, and the Chinese communities began producing more children, which helped ease the isolation of the various Chinatowns from the rest of society. These children took advantage of the American educational system, and a high percentage went on to earn college degrees. They were especially drawn to the sciences, accounting, engineering, drafting and college teaching. Today, the Chinese stand as an outstanding example of people who, despite government-sanctioned racism, have survived and prospered socially and economically.

THE IRISH

The Irish did not immigrate to the United States in significant numbers until the 1820s. These first Irish immigrants were mostly descendants of Ulster County Protestants who called themselves "Scotch-Irish." They had been trickling in since colonial times and were, for the most part, "skilled workers, small businessmen, and educated people."[31] They settled mainly in the Shenandoah Valley of Virginia and the Piedmont area of North and South Carolina and completely assimilated into the surrounding American population. When the Irish Catholics arrived later, the Scotch-Irish would have nothing to do with them and refused to be identified with them.

The Irish Catholics began significant immigration to the United States in the 1830s. Over the years the wealth of Ireland had been concentrated in a few hands, with the vast majority of the population left desperately poor, trying to survive on farms which contained only a few acres of land. Absentee landlords took the best the land produced—eggs, butter, bacon and flour—as rent, leaving the farmers and their families to survive on the proceeds from the potato crop. Despite the crushing poverty of the nation, its population swelled "to more than eight million in 1841, making Ireland the most densely populated country in Europe."[32] As things became worse, more and more of the young left Ireland for the United States.

In 1845 the potato blight hit Ireland, and for a nation whose people depended on the potato for survival, the results were disastrous. "The 1846 and 1847 crops failed completely, and those of 1848 and 1849 were but little better."[33] The potato blight did more than cause hardship; it caused mass death. "A million people died of starvation or starvation-related diseases and epidemics."[34] The international community tried to help Ireland, but the disaster was too vast for any amount of outside aid to alleviate. For millions of starving Irish, escaping the country was the only way of escaping death. The result was massive emigration, mostly to the United States.

Because of the terrible conditions in Ireland, the people who left were basically penniless, and so their trip to the United States was difficult and deadly. Most travelled in the holds of cargo ships which were overcrowded, filthy, had no toilet facilities, and provided only untreated river water to drink. Almost none of the ships carried any medical personnel, so medical problems went untreated. All of this extracted a terrible toll from the immigrants. "In the most disastrous year of all, 1847, about 20 percent of the huge famine immigration died en route to America or upon landing."[35] Even slave ships had a better record of survival than did the ships carrying the Irish immigrants. The average death rate on slave ships of the same period was about 9 percent.[36]

Though they were mostly from rural or small town areas, the Irish immigrants were so poor when they arrived that they tended to settle in their ports of entry, which for most meant either New York or Boston. Their non-urban backgrounds had not prepared them for urban living and they possessed few marketable skills. However, because of Ireland's long and mostly unhappy relationship with England, they did speak English, an advantage other immigrants did not have from the beginning. Also, because of their generations-long struggle with England, they had learned how to organize politically. The Catholic Church, which had become socially active in Ireland because of British oppression, became a rallying point and a source of strength for the Irish immigrants in the United States. Also, unlike general immigration patterns, where males immigrated first and sent for families later, the Irish immigrated as whole families, adding to the stability of the immigrant community from the beginning.

The Irish immigrants needed all the help they could get. Crowded into cramped quarters in the urban Northeast, life was difficult. Their neighborhoods were filthy and disease-ridden. Alcoholism and a tendency to become involved in fights gave the

Irish a bad reputation. Indeed, the terms "fighting Irish," "paddy wagon," and "Donnybrook" entered the English language because of the rough-and-tumble life in the Irish immigrant communities. Most worked as domestic servants or unskilled laborers. Irish unskilled laborers tended to be concentrated in backbreaking, dirty and dangerous jobs such as coal mining or canal and railroad building. "In the pre-Civil War South, Irish laborers were often used in work considered too dangerous for slaves."[37] Many could find no work and so were dependent on public charity, a fact which reinforced the popular concept of the Irish as inferior human beings.

Slowly the Irish moved beyond the port cities where they had been originally concentrated. By the 1870s, there were sizable Irish communities in Buffalo, Chicago, Milwaukee, New Orleans and San Francisco, in addition to the long established communities in New York and Boston. Though they quickly accumulated significant political power, economically they advanced rather slowly. They were slow to enter the skilled trades and white-collar professions and did not demonstrate a significant commitment to higher education. While many did rise to high levels of material success, the majority remained blue-collar workers.

After the first generation, the Irish began to assimilate quickly into the general population. They gradually became more educationally oriented and achieved representation in greater numbers in all the major professions. Although starting in total poverty and subject to the worst living conditions imaginable, looked down upon by almost all other Americans and having almost no marketable skills, the Irish, in the generations since their arrival, have proven themselves a valued part of what makes the United States great.

THE JAPANESE

The Japanese did not arrive in the United States until late in the nineteenth century. The traditionally isolationist policies of Japan had prevented earlier immigration. At first, Japanese immigration was only a trickle, with less than 400 arriving in the United States between 1860 and 1880. During the 1880s, there was a dramatic upswing as more than 2,000 arrived, and in the 1890s, more than 6,000. Between 1900 and 1910, the floodgates really opened and more than 100,000 Japanese immigrants arrived.[38] However, the restrictive immigration laws which were aimed at all Asians affected the Japanese, and by the 1920s the flood had been reduced to a trickle. The Japanese immigrant community was predominantly male, and many, after having spent some time in the United States, decided to return home.

Initially the Japanese were welcomed in the United States. Unlike other immigrants, the Japanese had been carefully selected by their government, which made sure that those who came to the United States were of good character and ambitious enough to overcome the obstacles which confront all immigrants. The Japanese began life in the United States as manual laborers. The majority found jobs as farm workers but many found work "in a variety of other strenuous laboring tasks on railroads and in mines, lumber mills, canneries, meat-packing plants, and similar arduous occupations. Some became personal servants to affluent Americans."[39] They were willing to work long, hard hours for low wages without complaining. When they worked jobs where they were paid on a piece-work basis they consistently earned much more than any other group. These very qualities earned them the hatred of organized labor, and they were even refused membership in local unions. Because of this opposition, many left the ranks of laborers and became tenant farmers (though some were able to buy land) and small businessmen so they could be their own bosses. This didn't help them avoid opposition. As farmers and small businessmen, they were in competition with their former employers, and those employers who loved the Japanese as employees feared and hated them as rivals. Since the Japanese were concentrated in several areas of California, they were quite visible in those areas and made convenient targets for the anti-Asian sentiment which had been growing since the 1870s.

The Chinese Exclusion Act of 1882 had barred Chinese, specifically, and Asians generally from becoming naturalized citizens. In 1913, California enacted the Alien Land Law which was aimed specifically at the Japanese. According to this law, only United States citizens could own California land and since the Japanese were barred from citizenship, they were barred from owning land. Californians lobbied Washington to forbid further Japanese immigration. Such a law probably would have passed had Japan been a weak nation but, "having defeated China in war in 1895 and Russia in 1905,"[40] the Japanese had to be respected. In 1905, the city of San Francisco's school board voted to segregate Japanese students. This decision was vigorously protested by the Japanese government. President Theodore Roosevelt convinced San Francisco to repeal the decision in exchange for an executive order limiting Japanese immigration. In the Gentlemen's Agreement of 1908, worked out between the two national governments, Japan "agreed not to issue visas to laborers bound for the United States."[41] The United States, for its part, agreed to allow wives to join their husbands who were already here and for parents and children to be reunited. This helped balance the Japanese immigrant community which had become heavily male and had separated many families.

There seemed to be no basis for all the fears Californians expressed regarding the Japanese. They were model citizens and hard workers, and their communities were clean, orderly and safe. They demonstrated all the qualities which were praised in other groups, and still they were besieged by hatred!

Despite hatred and harassment the Japanese persevered. The first generation, the *Issei*, moved into new areas of the economy. By 1930, the Japanese gardener was a common sight in California. Connected with Japanese success in agriculture was the rise of the Japanese produce market. "In Los Angeles, *Issei* owned dry cleaners, lunch counters, and fisheries as well as cheap hotels."[42] Because the *Issei* had worked so hard and saved so carefully, they were able to send their children, the second generation, or *Nisei*, to college, and from there the Japanese had an *entrée* to a variety of professions. Everything seemed to be going well for these industrious immigrants and their children.

When the Japanese attacked Pearl Harbor on Dec. 7, 1941, everything changed. The anger this attack aroused toward the government of Japan soon became anger expressed at Japanese-Americans. At first there were sporadic incidents of violence. This was followed by the detainment of approximately 1,500 Japanese suspected of being sympathetic with the government of Japan. This move, incidentally, was supported by most Japanese-Americans, who understood their delicate position in the United States. Anti-Japanese hysteria continued to grow, and finally in February, 1942, President Franklin Roosevelt "signed an Executive Order giving the army authority to evacuate 'any and all persons' from 'military areas' as designated by the army and to provide 'accommodations' for them elsewhere."[43] During the next ten months, about 110,000 Japanese were uprooted and taken to group compounds which were nothing more than concentration camps. Given almost no time to sell their property, they lost everything they had worked so hard to acquire. Upon their return from the camps, many found that even their bank accounts had disappeared. This action cost the Japanese community about 400,000,000 1942 dollars.[44] Not only was no act of sabotage ever traced to any Japanese-American, but some 30,000 served honorably in the military in World War II. As the war came to an end, they were gradually released from the camps to start life anew.

After World War II the second generation *Nisei* prospered. They put a high value on education, and many earned degrees in "engineering, optometry, or business administration."[45] The third generation, or *Sansei*, many of whom were born in the concentration camps, have continued the general upward mobility of the Japanese-Americans. The Japanese benefited from the post-World War II relaxation of immigration restraints against Asians and have continued to come to the United States in significant numbers. Some have come to make the United States their permanent home, and others have come temporarily to work for several years at the American branches of major Japanese corporations. In 1990, there were 847,562 Japanese in the United States, with over 60% living in two states, California and Hawaii. The Japanese-Americans, who suffered the worst American example of human rights violation outside of slavery, have had the courage and understanding to pick up the pieces and make many positive contributions to the nation which for so long held them in such deep suspicion.

THE MEXICANS

Mexicans are a very old and yet very new part of the ethnic picture in the United States. In 1845, Texas was annexed by the United States government, and in 1848, Mexico was forced to sign the Treaty of Guadalupe Hidalgo which transferred a huge area (roughly one third of the entire nation of Mexico) to United States control. This immense area, stretching from Kansas and Oklahoma westward to California, was populated by people whose culture was Mexican. They could not properly be called immigrants, because they never moved. The borders of their nation had moved. Yet they could not be called Americans, because they were totally separated from the mainstream of American culture. Since American property laws differed from Mexican property laws, many Mexicans were defrauded of their property and didn't have the knowledge necessary to seek legal redress. As a result, there are Mexican families in the Southwest who have a much longer family history in what is today known as the United States than the Anglos who tend to see them as foreigners.

While there was some immigration from Mexico before 1900, the numbers were small. Mexican immigration into the United States is a story told primarily in the twentieth century. It is a story which cannot be told with much preciseness because the government kept rather slipshod statistics on Mexican immigration for many years. The first wave of Mexican immigrants arrived in the United States between 1900 and 1930. Between 1910 and 1929, 685,000 Mexicans entered the United States.[46] The Mexican Revolution of 1910 and the depressed Mexican economy helped stimulate this first immigration. This group, for the most part, stayed near the Mexican border, though by 1930, there were small communities of Mexicans in Colorado and northern California.

These new immigrants were welcomed by many employers. Following the Chinese Exclusion Act of 1882 and the radical downturn in Chinese immigration it caused, many American employers lost a valuable source of cheap, dependable labor. To find a new source, they looked to the new Mexican immigrants. "Mexican-Americans were perceived as a pool of both expendable and exploitable workers that were close at hand."[47] Many worked for the railroads in construction or maintenance or as watchmen.

Others were migrant farm workers. Those who worked for the railroads and as farm workers tended to be isolated in small communities far removed from urban centers. Their living conditions were, by American standards, deplorable, and education for their children was almost nonexistent. A few Mexicans migrated to large urban areas and worked in factories. Americans in the Southwest generally looked down on these Mexican immigrants because of their poverty, their skin color, their work habits, the way they expressed their culture and their high rate of illiteracy. This hostility tended to isolate the Mexicans even more and severely reduced the rate at which any of them could move into the mainstream of American life.

Things took an ugly turn during the Depression which hit the United States in the fall of 1929. Because of the Depression, the Mexican population, by and large, was unemployed and dependent on government aid for their daily survival. This caused enormous anger among the general population, which was also suffering privation because of the Depression. In response to this situation, many local governments, aided by the federal government, "repatriated" (deported would be a more proper word) "about 400,000 Mexicans. This figure included a number of children who were American citizens because they had been born in the United States."[48]

There was another major influx of Mexicans during World War II. With large numbers of young men serving in the military, there were labor shortages in various fields. To ease this situation the United States government, in cooperation with the Mexican government, created the *Bracero* program which allowed Mexicans to obtain temporary work permits so they could become a part of the work force of the United States. What was supposed to be a temporary solution to a wartime labor shortage lasted until 1964. The program began on a modest scale as about 50,000 *Braceros* were recruited in 1945. By the late 1950s, there were more than 400,000 in the *Bracero* program, but by 1964, this had tapered off to just over 177,000.[49] This program gave many Mexicans their first taste of the good life in the United States. When the program ended, they kept coming, but now they were considered illegal aliens.

The pattern of Mexicans entering the United States illegally did not begin in 1964. By the 1920s thousands of Mexicans were being deported each year because they did not have the proper documents. With the end of the *Bracero* program, the undocumented alien problem began to increase dramatically. By the 1970s, it had gotten so out of hand that no one had the slightest idea of its dimensions. In 1979, the Mexican government estimated the number of their citizens who were undocumented aliens at between 480,000 and 1.22 million. However, in 1978, the Population Office of the City Planning Department of New York had estimated the total illegal population (including Mexican and others) of New York City to be 750,000. Some have estimated that there were as many as twelve million undocumented aliens in the United States in the early 1980s.[50] The best estimate seems to be that there were from three to five million undocumented aliens in the early 1980s, with the majority being Mexican. The irony of it all is that several times during the 1980s, the INS discovered that it had employees who were undocumented. The undocumented alien problem has been and continues to be a thorny problem for the United States government.

The Immigration Reform and Control Act of 1986, which sought to provide anmesty and citizenship to part of the undocumented population, along with greater penalties for employing undocumented aliens, has done little to solve the overall problem. If it has any significant effect on the future of the undocumented situation, it will probably be to inspire both the undocumented and those who seek to hire them to create inventive strategies to circumvent the law. The undocumented alien story, a story not well understood by most North Americans, is a part of a larger story. From the beginning of their immigration, many Mexicans wanted to come to the United States for a while to be with family or to work and make some money and then return to Mexico. Since the 1920s, there has been an enormous back-and-forth movement across the United States—Mexican border which has, for the most part, eluded United States law enforcement programs designed to stop it. The fine points of United States immigration legislation has meant little to those involved in this back-and-forth movement.

During World War II and after, the tension between the general North American population and the Mexican-American population remained. There were many incidents, the most remembered of which is probably the so called "Zoot Suit riots" which occurred in Los Angeles in 1943 and pitted North American sailors against Mexican-American youths in violent street riots.

In the 1940s there was an upswing in Mexican immigration, which "was less than two thousand in 1940, but was more than six thousand by 1944, and was nearly ten thousand by 1952. From there on, the rise was even sharper. In 1956 more than 65,000 Mexican immigrants entered the United States."[51] But this was only the beginning. After a few years in which immigration from Mexico declined slightly, a new and larger wave began. Many in Mexico were still trapped in hopeless poverty while just across the border immense wealth was available—and everybody knew it. Also, there was a trend toward industrialization in the Mexican economy, much of it fueled by North American companies going south to find cheap labor. These new factories acquainted Mexicans with job skills which could earn them much more money in the United States, so as soon as they could, many of Mexico's industrial workers immigrated legally or illegally to the United States. The more generous immigration legislation of 1965 also benefited Mexicans wishing to come north. Then there was the presence of the established Mexican-American communities, various social agencies, and an activist Catholic Church to encourage new Mexican immigration. All of these not only encouraged new legal immigrants but also gave support to and championed the cause of undocumented aliens.

In the 1960s and 70s the pace of Mexican immigration quickened. In 1965, almost 38,000 Mexicans arrived in the United States. In 1975, the year's total was over 62,000, and in 1978, over 92,000. The decade of the 1970s saw over 600,000 new Mexican immigrants enter the United States.[52] These immigrants were not the desperately poor of Mexico nor were they well off. They had an educational level of near or even above the Mexican national average and they were aquainted with urban life. In the 1980s, Mexican immigration reached its highest level in history, and by 1990, there were 13,495,938 Mexican-Americans in the United

States. California, Texas, Arizona, and New Mexico have the largest numbers of Mexican-Americans with smaller communities developing in Denver, Kansas City, Chicago, Detroit, and New York City.

The Mexican immigrant community is still, by and large, functioning separately from mainstream North American culture, but since so many are so new to this country and since many do not intend to stay here permanently, this is to be expected. The Mexican immigrants who came early in the twentieth century have begun to move out into the mainstream. They are approaching the national average in economic standing but still lag behind in educational levels and representation in the professions which require post-graduate degrees. A number of Mexican-Americans have achieved fame in the fields of sports and entertainment. Mexican-Americans will be an increasingly important ethnic group, especially in the Southwest. Forming a positive working relationship between Anglo-Americans and Mexican-Americans is important for both groups. Such a relationship holds the key to the social and economic future of the Southwest.

THE KOREANS

The first Koreans to immigrate to the United States were a few students and some political refugees who arrived around 1900. About the same time, several thousand Koreans had been recruited to work in Hawaiian sugar plantations. Nearly one thousand of these eventually came to the West Coast of the United States. Anti-Asian activists were as opposed to Koreans as they were to Chinese and Japanese, and they successfully lobbied the government to restrict Korean immigration. After the Gentlemen's Agreement of 1908, which put tight restrictions on Korean as well as Japanese immigration, only a trickle of Koreans, mainly students and political refugees, continued to come to the United States. Several thousand students came after 1945, but even after World War II there was still no significant Korean community in the United States. After the Korean War, North American soldiers who had married Koreans were permitted to bring their brides home, and this added somewhat to the total Korean immigrant community. However, these war brides were dispersed through the country and seldom functioned as part of any Korean community. From 1960 to 1965 a few thousand more entered.

The beginning of significant Korean immigration was made possible by the Immigration Act of 1965. Taking advantage of the provisions in that legislation, Koreans began arriving in significant numbers. In 1969, more than 6,000 Koreans came to the United States, and in 1977, more than 30,000 came. All told, between 1965 and 1980, around 250,000 Koreans came to the United States.[53] The 1980s saw Korean immigration increase dramatically, and by 1990, there were 798,849 Koreans in the United States.

Los Angeles received the largest number of Korean immigrants. Most of them settled near an area called Koreatown and established a vibrant community with community service organizations, churches, newspapers, and radio and television stations. Christian churches played an important role in the Korean community, Korea having a higher percentage of Christians than any other Asian nation. Sizable Korean communities also were established in New York City and Chicago. The New York and Chicago Koreans were more scattered and did not form the kind of cohesive community the Los Angeles Koreans did. In the early 1980s, a sizable Korean community began forming in central Orange County, California, and opened hundreds of businesses on Garden Grove Boulevard in Garden Grove.

Some of the most visible Koreans were those who came to the United States trained as doctors and nurses. Many Koreans opened small businesses such as restaurants, grocery stores, and, especially in New York City, produce markets. Korean businesses thrived in part because they could keep their overhead, and thus their prices, low by using family members rather than hired help as their employees. Gradually, they have moved into a wide variety of businesses such as fast food franchises, clothing, furniture, liquor, and video stores. The Koreans have proven to be aggressive, industrious, upwardly mobile people. They have revitalized older business areas which were dying before they arrived. In some urban areas, however, there has been significant tension between the Korean and Black communities. At times, this tension has produced violence. Koreans have placed a high value on education and seem to be heading for the same kind of social, professional, and economic success which has been achieved by the Chinese and Japanese. "In one survey of all residents of the United States who had completed at least four years of college, those of Korean background led all the rest with 36.3 percent."[54]

THE FILIPINOS

Filipinos began arriving in the United States in the first decade of the twentieth century. This country's relationship with the Philippine Islands dated from the Spanish-American War. Before the United States arrived on the scene, Spain had controlled the Islands for over 330 years, beginning during the reign of King Philip II, after whom the country was named. In the late 1800s, José Rizal led a resistance movement which sought to end Spanish rule of the islands. Shortly after Rizal's execution on Dec. 31, 1896, leadership of the resistance passed to Emilio Aguinaldo. He assisted North American forces in expelling the Spanish from the Philippines in 1898. When the Treaty of Paris was ratified in 1899, it transferred control of the Philippines from Spain to the United States. Aguinaldo was furious, saying he had been promised that his nation would be independent, but the United States denied that any such promise had been made. The result was that Aguinaldo led an insurrection against North American rule which lasted until 1901.

Despite the opposition which many Filipinos expressed to North American rule, it did have one very important effect. All Filipinos were considered United States nationals and, as such, could freely and with no quota restrictions travel to the United States and all of its territories. The first Filipinos to come to the United States were students who came to receive a college education. They began arriving in 1903 under the so-called "*Pensionado*" program. The idea was to give these young Filipinos a United States education and then send them back home to bring North American expertise, learning and a commitment to democracy to the Philippines. The program was only partly successful, for some of these United States-educated Filipinos soon began to question the American domination of their homeland. Many young Filipinos were inspired by the "*Pensionados*" to go to the United States and seek a college education on their own. Many of these independent students failed to achieve their goals. Some returned home, while others stayed in this country and took unskilled jobs.

A second wave of Filipinos left their homeland to seek work, not an education. Many Filipinos in rural areas were anxious to leave the country "because of growing poverty, lack of available land, and increasing farm tenancy."[55] Many were recruited to work in the sugar plantations of Hawaii. In the past, the Hawaiian sugar planters had relied on Chinese, Japanese, and Korean immigrants to work their plantations. United States law now banned immigration from these countries, and so the planters looked to the Filipinos, who could freely immigrate in unlimited numbers, as replacement workers. Others migrated to Alaska to work in the salmon canneries. Recruiters from several steamship companies travelled throughout the Philippines telling of the good life in the United States and urging people to book passage so they could have their dreams of wealth come true.

At first, immigration to the United States was slow. By 1910, the New Orleans area, with 109, had the largest concentration of Filipinos in North America and there were only 5 Filipinos in California. By 1920, there were nearly 4,000 on the Pacific coast of the United States and in Alaska. Between 1920 and 1930, 45,000 more arrived. Most of them stayed in California and that state's "Filipino population increased about 91 percent in the 1920s."[56] Others moved east to "Chicago, Detroit, New York, and Philadelphia."[57]

Most of the Filipino immigrants were young, single males. They had come to make their fortunes in the United States and then return to the Philippines as wealthy men. Because of this, they had little interest in fitting into North American life and little regard for how they were perceived by society at large. Most of them spoke little English, had very poor job skills and almost no education, and were ill prepared to deal with the racial prejudice they encountered when they arrived. Because of these factors, they had few employment options. A large number worked as migrant farm laborers. They went to the interior valleys of California and "soon dominated asparagus cutting; thinning and picking lettuce, strawberries, and sugar beets; and potato harvesting."[58] Others

worked as seamen on merchant marine vessels and some enlisted in
the United States Navy.

Before they came to the United States, most Filipinos had
heard of the wages paid in the United States and assumed that they
could get rich quickly. They had not understood the high cost of
living in the United States. Once here, they found that it took
everything they earned just to survive. Most found only seasonal
work and, when unemployed, drifted into the "Little Manilas" of
Los Angeles, San Francisco, and Stockton, California. In the cities,
some found work in menial hotel and restaurant jobs and as
domestic servants. Employers liked the Filipinos, for they did not
complain about hard work, long hours, and low pay.

It wasn't long before anti-Filipino sentiment began to rise
on the West Coast. Since Filipino farm workers accepted lower
wages than any other group, other groups of farm workers
expressed much hostility toward them. Once established as farm
workers, they began demanding higher wages, and when the
growers refused they would strike at critical times in the harvest,
thus earning them the hatred of many growers. Organized labor was
bitterly opposed to the Filipinos. The unions accused the Filipinos
of driving down wages and taking jobs away from whites. Others
saw them as savages and denounced them as "only one jump from
the jungle."[59] The Filipinos frequently patronized "taxi-dance" halls
where young women, mostly white, would dance with anyone who
would pay ten cents a minute. This raised fears that Filipino men
endangered white women. Filipinos "were frequently denied service
in restaurants and barber shops and barred from swimming pools,
movies and tennis courts."[60] They were accused of being a danger
to the public health and it was reported that Filipino babies were
born with parasites in their intestines. They were portrayed as being
hopelessly addicted to alcohol, gambling, sexual misconduct and
violence. Though statistics proved "that between 1919 and 1929,
the Filipino crime profile was the same as that of whites and
blacks,"[61] anti-Filipino leaders consistently portrayed Filipinos as
a major crime problem. Filipino Christians complained that while
white Christians would befriend them at church functions, those
same Christians would ignore them in public. Between 1926 and
1934, there were repeated incidents of violence involving whites

and Filipinos. Anti-Filipino leaders demanded that Congress bar Filipinos from the United States, but since Filipinos were nationals, this could not be done.

What no legislation could do, the Depression did. The collapse of the United States economy drastically reduced the flow of Filipinos to the United States. In 1934, the Tydings-McDuffie Act, which set up the process for granting independence to the Philippines, also set a quota of 50 per year for new Filipinos coming to the United States. Finally, on July 4, 1946, the Philippines received its independence and was allowed a quota of 100 immigrants a year.

The door to significant immigration did not open until the Immigration Act of 1965 was passed. Family reunification provisions in this act helped many Filipinos join family members already here. It also resolved the heavy male-female imbalance in the Filipino community. In the Philippines, the corruption of the Marcos government and its suspension of civil liberties, a protracted conflict with the communists who wanted to seize power and the Moros who wanted their independence, and a failing economy, all fueled increased emigration from the country. Many who came to the United States during the 1970s and 1980s were highly educated professionals such as teachers, accountants, engineers, physicians, nurses, pharmacists, and dentists. In 1970, there were 343,062 Filipinos in the United States, and in 1980, there were 774,640. In 1990, the Filipino population stood at 1,406,472, with more than half living in California. Though their history in this country has been difficult, they are emerging today as a group which is making valuable contributions to many areas of our society.

THE PUERTO RICANS

Puerto Rico was one of the first places in the New World to be colonized by Europeans. In 1508, Ponce de Leon claimed the island for Spain, a claim that would shape Puerto Rico's history for nearly four hundred years. Most of the native population "died of exhaustion, maltreatment, and diseases contracted from the Spaniards, for which the Indians had not developed biological immunity."[62] African slaves were then imported to work the mines and farms which the Spanish were developing. Because of the intermixture of Spanish, African, and Indian peoples, Puerto Rico has a rich cultural and racial heritage.

From the early 1800's, Puerto Rico yearned for independence and was finally given limited autonomy by Spain in 1897. This autonomy was short-lived. In 1898, Spain was forced to cede the country to the United States as part of the price for losing the Spanish-American War. As a colony of the United States, it was first ruled by the military and then by a civilian government controlled by Washington. The Jones Act of 1917 granted citizenship to Puerto Ricans, which meant that they, like the Filipinos, could come to the mainland without the hinderance of immigration quotas.

Gradually, the country was allowed greater and greater autonomy until it achieved Commonwealth status. "In 1947, Puerto Ricans were granted the right to elect their own governor, and in 1948, Luis Muñoz Marín became the first elected governor of the island. In 1952, Puerto Ricans achieved the right to make their own constitution."[63] Its Commonwealth status means that while the democratically elected Puerto Rican government structures its own internal affairs, ultimate legislative authority lies in the United States Congress.

Between 1898 and 1944, fewer than 100,000 Puerto Ricans immigrated to the United States. Many of those earlier immigrants came as a result of the Depression which crippled the sugar industry, the main industry of the island. Following World War II, there was a dramatic upturn in Puerto Rican immigration. There were three reasons for this upturn. First was a United States sponsored program of economic development called Operation Bootstrap. While it assisted Puerto Rico's urban and industrial development, it did not provide enough new jobs to keep up with the rapid population increase of the island. This resulted in a major unemployment problem. Many left with the hope of finding jobs in the United States. Second, with the advent of cheap air transportation, the trip to the United States was within reach of much of the population. Third, there was a shortage of unskilled laborers in the factories along the east coast of the United States.

Labor recruiters encouraged Puerto Ricans to come north, fill those jobs and enjoy limitless prosperity.

And so they came, by the thousands and then the tens of thousands. "Thirteen thousand came over in 1945 alone, and this more than tripled in 1946."[64] By the early 1950's, there were over 50,000 a year coming to live in the United States. By 1970, "there were a million Puerto Ricans in New York"[65] City alone, with significant but dramatically smaller communities in Chicago, Philadelphia, and Newark. Hundreds of thousands more came for a brief stay and then returned home. Those who stayed found employment in a variety of low paying professions. "The men became 'pressers and floor boys in garment factories, dishwashers, bus boys, pantrymen, laundry workers [and] porters'; the women were likely to end up as 'domestics, in hospitals, and in laundries . . . as hand sewers, floor girls, cleaners, [and] sewing-machine operators.'"[66] In New York City there was a shortage of affordable housing in the 1950's, and many Puerto Ricans, owing to their meager wages, were forced to live in apartments which were vermin-infested and lacked adequate plumbing and heating. This was a problem other new immigrants had faced in years past. The Puerto Ricans did have one advantage earlier groups lacked. By the time they began arriving in significant numbers, the United States welfare system was largely in place and provided them much-needed assistance as they struggled to establish themselves in their new country. Determined to find a new and better life, they kept coming north; by 1990, the United States Puerto Rican population was 2,727,754, mostly concentrated in the northeast.

Their reception in the United States was mixed. The light-complexioned Puerto Ricans found a higher level of acceptance and a broader range of opportunities than those with a dark complexion. Anglo society regarded the dark-skinned Puerto Ricans as Blacks, and this limited both their acceptance and their economic and social opportunities.

Gradually they moved up the economic ladder. Soon Puerto Ricans were operating small businesses such as "barbershops, cleaning establishments, lunch counters, beauty parlors, radio repair shops, and groceries."[67] They have been slow to participate in the political life of the nation and have developed few ethnic social and religious organizations which could advance their interests. Many observers feel that this is because of the great back-and-forth movement of Puerto Ricans between their homeland and the United States. This continued contact has led the first generation to continue to feel more a part of Puerto Rico than of the United States. While the second generation is participating more actively in United States life than the first, Puerto Ricans still maintain a strong sense of ethnic separateness from the rest of the population. They are still a very new part of the American mosaic and are still trying to find their place.

THE CUBANS

On January 1, 1959, when Fidel Castro assumed control of Cuba, a new chapter in the history of ethnic groups in the United States began. From 1959 to the present, refugees more than immigrants have shaped the ethnic character of the United States. The country had been receiving refugees long before 1959. It had received significant numbers of European refugees in the aftermath of World War II and following the unsuccessful Hungarian revolution of 1956. It had also received many Chinese refugees after the Communist came to power in China in 1949. These refugees were only a foretaste of what was to come.

The refugee flow in the immediate aftermath of Fidel Castro taking power in Cuba was not all that great, but it accelerated quickly and "reached flood proportions just prior to the Cuban missile crisis of October, 1962. By then 3,000 persons weekly were arriving from Cuba."[68] All told, the first great wave of Cuban refugees, which Castro halted after the missile crisis, amounted to about 200,000 people.

From late 1962 until 1965, only about 9,000 refugees came from Cuba.[69] Most of them came in rickety boats and at great personal risk. These refugees came with almost no money, and federal funds were eventually appropriated to aid in their settlement. A number of pieces of legislation were passed dealing with the issues brought up by this large influx of refugees, but no cohesive approach was developed for dealing with refugees. Many seemed to think that we would never again see as many refugees flooding into the United States as we saw in the aftermath of the Communists' rise to power in Cuba.

Many of the Cubans who fled just before or in the three years following Castro's revolution were officials in the Batista government which was overthrown by Castro. Others were supporters of Batista or disenchanted followers of Castro. They tended to be white, highly educated professionals from the middle and upper classes of society. Miami, Florida, and its surrounding areas quickly became the center of the Cuban refugee community, with about half of the total refugee population living there. Cuban refugee communities also emerged in New York City, New Jersey, and several other Northeastern cities. The CIA recruited several thousand Cuban refugees to participate in the unseccessful Bay of Pigs invasion in April, 1961.

In December, 1965, Castro allowed resumption of the airlift of refugees out of Cuba, and another sizable group came to the United States. These people tended to be poorer and less educated than the first group and had more difficulty adapting to life in the United States. By the mid-1970s, the refugee flood from Cuba had dwindled to a trickle.

In 1980, Castro faced the prospect of dealing with large numbers of his people who wanted to leave the country. After a diplomatic fiasco at the Peruvian embassy in Cuba concerning people wanting to leave, Castro suddenly announced, on April 18, that anyone who wanted to leave was free to go. They had to do so immediately and they had to go directly to the country where they wanted to settle. This allowed for no screening of refugees. Almost all wanted to go to the United States. On April 21 the first boatloads of refugees began to leave the Cuban port of Mariel, heading for the United States.

The United States government did not have an established procedure for dealing with this flood of refugees. At first, President Carter could not decide whether to accept the refugees or not, but the decision was eventually made to accept all who came. However, after 130,000 had arrived, the government changed its mind and refused to accept any more. The Mariel refugees were not well accepted even by the Cuban refugees who had arrived previously. They tended to be a mixed lot. They were mostly young, working class males who had little education and few marketable job skills. There were also some, though the number was vastly exaggerated by some critics, who were criminals or mentally ill. These undesirables became a point of contention between Cuba and the United States and finally, in December of 1984, the two governments signed an agreement to return the undesirables to Cuba.

All told, some 800,000 Cuban refugees came to the United States between 1959 and 1985.[70] In 1990, the Cuban population of the United States stood at 1,043,932 and was concentrated mostly in Florida and New York. Their community is still so new that little can be said about how they will, in the long run, fare in their new land. They seem determined to become a positive factor in life in the United States.

With the downfall of Communism in Eastern Europe and the Soviet Union, many Cuban-Americans are hopeful of the imminent collapse of the Castro government. If this happens, a significant number of Cubans may decide to leave the United States and return to Cuba. Such a turn of events would almost surely cause great turmoil in many Cuban families, with some members wishing to return "home" to Cuba and others wishing to stay "home" in the United States.

THE CENTRAL AND SOUTH AMERICANS

While the Mexicans are the largest of the groups to immigrate to the United States from south of the border, all of the countries of Central and South America are represented in our current population. Most, but not all, could be called Hispanic, but even the countries which might properly be labeled "Hispanic" have their own unique historical, social and cultural flavor. A detailed discussion of each country is beyond the scope of this book, but a few brief observations will be made in order to give a taste of the diversity of Central and South America.

"From the Rio Grande to Cape Horn, Latin America measures 7,000 miles."[71] Most of the people of this area are concentrated within 400 miles from the coast with the interior being sparsely populated. While Europeans settled throughout the area, most of them "migrated to the thinly settled plains of the southern part of the continent."[72] Elevation and proximity to the coast play important roles in the basic life orientation of the people. "The people of the highlands tend to be reserved and introverted, suspicious and active; they give a general impression of sadness. The people along the coast are outgoing, extroverted, imaginative and give a general impression of happiness. A resident of Mexico City, 7,000 feet above sea level, is more like a resident of Bogota, 9,000 feet high, although they are thousands of miles apart, than he is like a person from Veracruz, 280 miles from Mexico City but on the coast."[73]

Twenty countries make up Central and South America. Sixteen fit into the category we call Hispanic. They are Costa Rica, El Salvador, Guatemala, Honduras, Nicaragua, Panama, Venezuela, Colombia, Ecuador, Peru, Chile, Bolivia, Paraguay, Argentina, Uruguay and Brazil. (Mexico, although Hispanic, is geographically a part of North America.) Some of these, owing to unique historical circumstances, have been less influenced by Hispanic culture than others. "The countries of the Southern Cone (Argentina, Uruguay, and to a lesser extent Chile) have the most European population, made up largely of the descendants of European migrants. Other countries, such as those in the Andean zone and much of Central America, have large indigenous populations or populations of mixed descent. In . . . Brazil the black population is more numerous, and its influence more important culturally."[74]

Brazil, by far the largest of the Hispanic countries, has additional areas of uniqueness. It has a Portuguese background and has had a history of social and political stability that is unique to the area. Politically, it progressed with relatively little turmoil from a Portuguese colony to an independent empire to a republic. The Roman Catholic church has had less influence on the history of Brazil than it has had in other countries of the area and this has allowed for rapid secularization of the society. All in all Brazil prides itself in the fact that it has gone its own way socially, culturally, and politically and resents being lumped together with all the other Hispanic countries.

Four countries—Belize, lying east of Guatemala, and Guyana, Suriname, and French Guiana, situated on the northeastern shoulder of South America—are culturally and socially connected with the islands of the Caribbean. Belize is strongly connected to Great Britain culturally and politically. English is the language of education, but Creole English, Carib, and Maya are also spoken. In northern Belize, Spanish predominates. Guyana is connected politically and cultually to both Great Britain and Holland. Both English and Creole English are spoken by the people. The population includes the descendants of ex-slaves from Africa, a large group from the subcontinent of India, along with those of German, Irish, Maltese, Portuguese, and Chinese ancestry. Suriname has strong Dutch influences along with some British. The official language is Dutch, but three English-related Creole dialects are also spoken. As with other nations of the Caribbean, the descendants of African slaves make up a sizable part of the population. East Indians, Chinese, West Indians from Barbados, Portuguese, Javanese, and Indonesians add variety to the population. Because of a strong Indonesian presence, Suriname has been shaped, in part, by Moslem culture. French Guiana shows strong French influence in culture, education and economy. French and French Creole are the languages spoken by the people.

This brief overview demonstrates that one must be quite careful not to ignore the rich and diverse cultural, political and social heritage of Central and South America.

THE VIETNAMESE

In 1965, the year in which the United States dramatically relaxed restrictions on Asian immigration, President Lyndon Johnson escalated the war in Vietnam. Many still thought the war could be won, but as the sixties became the seventies the War became more and more costly to fight and was increasingly unpopular with large segments of the American population. Eventually, it was decided to withdraw American troops from South Vietnam and provide money and hardware so the South Vietnamese could continue to pursue the war. The policy was a dismal failure, and by early 1975, almost everyone knew that it was only a matter of time before the Viet Cong and their North Vietnamese allies would conquer the south. As Communist troops closed in on Saigon, tens of thousands of people poured into the city. Utter chaos ruled. On April 30, the city fell without a major defense effort ever having been attempted.

In the spring of 1975, few considered the possibility of massive numbers of Vietnamese immigrating to the United States. Prior to 1975, a few Vietnamese had immigrated and a number of soldiers from this country had brought Vietnamese spouses home with them. As the end neared, the South Vietnamese government, encouraged by the American government, organized an airlift of orphans to the United States. In early April of 1975, United States government representatives were saying that their "first priority was to remove American citizens and their dependents, numbering slightly more than 4,000."[75] In addition to this number, government officials said they only planned to evacuate some 17,600 Vietnamese who had worked for the United States government.[76] Just before the fall of Saigon, however, the government agreed to help evacuate all Vietnamese who, at any time, had worked for the United States, along with all their dependents. Saigon fell before any plans could be made to carry out this evacuation and in the end everything degenerated into panic and confusion. Somehow, in spite of the chaotic circumstances, the United States government was able to evacuate 52,000 Vietnamese before the Communists took the city.[77] In the aftermath of South Vietnam's collapse, desperate Vietnamese tried everything imaginable to get out of the country before the Communists could consolidate their control.

In the United States there was major opposition to allowing a significant number of Vietnamese into the country. In 1975, both the Gallup and Harris organizations found a majority of Americans opposed to the idea of accepting Vietnamese refugees. For many, their reasons for opposing the acceptance of Vietnamese were economic rather than racial. They were afraid the Vietnamese would take jobs away from Americans, and the mid-seventies were difficult years for the economy even without any new population influx. Finally, President Ford announced that he would admit 130,000 Vietnamese refugees. Four military bases were used to accommodate the refugees while they awaited resettlement. They were "Camp Pendleton, California; Fort Chafee, Arkansas; Eglin Air Force Base, Florida; and Fort Indian Town Gap, Pennsylvania."[78] The goal was to scatter the refugees throughout the country, but the majority eventually settled in California. By the end of 1975, all 130,000 refugees were settled. A few more refugees arrived in 1976 and 1977, but not many.

In 1978, events occurred which produced another flood of Vietnamese refugees. The Communist government of Vietnam moved to eliminate the business class as it began to reshape the economy into an orthodox communist mold. This caused much of the business class, most of whom were ethnic Chinese, to flee. Vietnam's war with China produced still more refugees. There were also bloody conflicts in Laos and Cambodia adding to the woes of Southeast Asia. "In August of 1978, the number of Vietnamese seeking asylum elsewhere in Asia averaged about 6,000 per month, but by the spring of 1979, it reached 65,000 monthly."[79] People were leaving by any means possible. Many made their way to Thailand, while others left by boat. Many suffered enormous hardship and violence as they fled. Initially, the United States government said it would accept an additional 15,000 Indochinese refugees, but by early 1979, it was accepting 7,000 a month, and that number grew to 14,000 a month by June. By 1985, the program which initially was designed to accept 130,000 had accepted around 700,000 Indochinese, with the vast majority being Vietnamese.[80] In 1990, there were 614,547 Vietnamese in the United States.

The first wave of Vietnamese refugees tended to be an elite group who were well educated and urban. Many were white collar workers or even professionals. They tended to be Catholic, they knew English, and they were rather well aquainted with American culture. This group had all the basic tools needed to succeed in the United States, and many of them did.

The second wave, in 1978 and after, contained many ethnic Chinese who had been in business in South Vietnam, and these, too, tended to do well. This second wave also contained many of the so-called "boat people." They were rural, uneducated, unaquainted with American culture and had no marketable job skills. They have had much difficulty adapting to life in the United States.

About one third of all Vietnamese refugees settled in California. The second largest concentration is in Texas, mostly in

Houston and along the Gulf Coast. Other centers are in "Virginia, Louisiana, New York, Pennsylvania, Minnesota, Oregon, Washington, and Illinois."[81]

Differences between the cultures of Vietnam and the United States have caused friction in some areas where the Vietnamese have settled. There has been considerable friction between the Vietnamese and the Black and Mexican communities. Blacks and Mexicans have contended that Vietnamese were taking jobs, housing, and government aid away from them. There have also been violent confrontations between Vietnamese and others involved in the fishing industry along the Gulf Coast of Texas.

Despite the tragedies of the past and the misunderstandings and hostility of the present, the Vietnamese appear to be moving along the same lines as other, more established, ethnic groups. Those who were adults when they arrived in the United States are very ethnically conscious. The children are very Americanized, sometimes to the dismay of their parents. They have developed social organizations and business communities to serve their daily needs. While the adults work hard at their jobs or in their businesses, the children work hard and excel in school. Beginning only a few years ago with almost nothing and facing much hostility, the Vietnamese have already come a long way toward becoming an integral part of the North American ethnic mosaic.

THE CONTINUING AMERICAN MOSAIC

This, then, is a part of the grand North American mosaic of people. The English, Germans, Black Africans, West Indians, Jews, Chinese, Irish, Japanese, Mexicans, Koreans, Filipinos, Cubans, and Vietnamese are just a few of the hundreds of people groups who are today a part of the population of the United States. The new immigrant and refugee groups of today do not mark a new development in the history of this country. They continue a historical reality that dates back to the early 1600s. Many of the recent immigrants and refugees are non-white, and that is a difference from earlier trends. We can choose to fracture this nation along racial lines or we can choose to celebrate the greatness of the American people, a people which today contains all the colors of God's human rainbow.

SIMILARITIES BETWEEN THE OLDER AND NEWER GROUPS

There are many similarities between the way the older groups and newer groups have related and are still relating to the North American experience. New groups have usually gathered in communities where they could be with their own kind. They have spoken their native language, developed businesses which catered to their unique needs, and created organizations which preserved their culture. Each has, over time, become a part of the mainstream United States. Some, in doing this, have maintained strong ethnic identity and others have almost completely assimilated into the culture of the United States. There seem to be several ways in which ethnic groups can deal with their ethnicity and their new identity as North Americans. We would be wise, as a nation and as the church, to let each group decide how it wants to fit into the North American mosaic.

DIFFERENCES BETWEEN THE OLDER AND NEWER GROUPS

There are also some significant differences between the older groups and the newer groups. While each of the older groups had its own culture, they were all based on a common Greco-Roman historical and cultural heritage. When they arrived in the United States, they encountered a culture that, while different from theirs in many ways, still shared their basic cultural foundations. This common cultural frame of reference helped make the newcomers and those already here reasonably comfortable with each other and fostered positive social contacts. The newer groups have come from cultures profoundly different from European culture, such as the various Asian and African cultures, or from cultures that have profoundly altered European culture, such as the Hispanic. When they arrived in the United States, they could find few points of contact with the dominant culture. This lack of a common cultural frame of reference has caused discomfort both for the newcomers and those already here and has led to considerable social misunderstanding and in some cases violence.

The older groups have come mostly from a Judeo-Christian religious tradition, and that is the major spiritual tradition they encountered here. Many of the newer groups, especially those from Asia and Africa have come from spiritual traditions far removed from the Judeo-Christian tradition. Americans have tended to react negatively to people whose religion they consider "heathen" or "savage."

The older groups, with the exception of Black slaves, have been mainly caucasian, while the newer groups have been mainly people of color. Owing to a longstanding prejudice in the United States against darker-skinned people, these new groups face problems of acceptance. Also, many of the new groups have come with their own prejudices against Anglos. This has caused difficulties.

For a variety of reasons the older groups shed their cultural and language distinctives relatively quickly. The newer groups, again for a variety of reasons, appear to be determined to keep their cultural and language distinctives for the foreseeable future. This makes interrelationships between them and the dominant culture somewhat difficult.

What all of this means for the church is that it cannot structure its ministry to today's immigrants and refugees the way it did a generation ago. All ministry with today's immigrants and refugees, if it is to be fruitful, must be cross-cultural ministry. This means the church must learn a whole new set of rules and realities as she ministers to today's newcomers. Some of those rules and realities will be introduced in chapter two of this book.

COMPARING IMMIGRANTS AND REFUGEES

Throughout its history, the United States has received both immigrants and refugees. In many ways, the two groups have had similar experiences as they have dealt with life in the United States. There are, however, significant differences between these two groups. If the church is to minister with maximum efficiency, she must become sensitive to these differences. Immigrants came to the United States because they freely chose to leave their country of origin. Refugees came because they were forced out or had to flee for their lives. Immigrant populations were usually, in the beginning, mainly young and male. These young males had come to see if this country could provide the kind of home they wanted for their families and to establish themselves economically so that they could provide for their families when they did come. Refugee populations have tended to include whole families. Family members who were left behind were seldom seen again. Whole families had to start anew, and this involved great difficulty. Immigrant families, once here, were anxious to become Americans and regarded North America as their permanent home. Refugee families often long to return to the country from which they fled, and so have been less willing to become Americanized. Immigrants have tended, for the most part, not to become quickly involved in politics in the United States. Their main concerns have revolved around establishing themselves economically. They also have quickly lost interest in the political questions confronting their country of origin. Refugees have tended to be highly involved in politics immediately upon their arrival. They have hoped to influence United States policy toward their homeland in such a way as to change things so they could return. For immigrants, the circumstances surrounding their departure from their homeland has tended to have a minimal effect upon their new life. For refugees, the horrors they have seen and experienced as they fled their homeland can haunt them for a lifetime and can negatively influence their ability to function in United States society. Immigrants have usually come from the lower strata of society and have come to the United States to improve their lot in life. Many refugees, especially those fleeing Communism, have been wealthy and educated and have settled for a lower standard of living in the United States so they could live in freedom. All of these differences need to be taken into consideration as we work with immigrants and refugees.

THREE TYPES OF IMMIGRANTS AND REFUGEES

Many North Americans persist in believing that the words of Emma Lazarus which are inscribed on the pedestal of the Statue of Liberty describe all immigrants and refugees—"Give me your tired, your poor, Your huddled masses . . . The wretched refuse of your teeming shores."[82] They have, thus, thought of all immigrants and refugees as poverty stricken, illiterate, lacking in job skills and unable, at first, to cope with life in the United States. Actually, there is a great deal of economic and educational diversity in most immigrant and refugee groups. We would be well advised to be sensitive to this diversity.

There are three major classifications which are helpful in getting a handle on the diversity within immigrant and refugee groups. First, the *labor* immigrants. These people come with little formal education and few job skills, and they fill the menial jobs in our society which generally pay minimum wage or only slightly more. While they seem miserably poor to most Americans, they are actually doing rather well when compared to the situation in their country of origin. Many eventually move into the American lower-middle class but many also remain in poverty and others gradually slip into welfare dependency.

Second, the *entrepreneurial* immigrants. These are people who are "skilled in what sociologist Franklin Frazier called 'the art of buying and selling.'"[83] They open small businesses which, at first, tend to serve the unique needs of their ethnic community. However, soon these entrepreneurs find a niche to fill in the larger community. Both the Korean and Cuban communities have a strong entrepreneurial immigrant presence. Some of these entrepreneurial immigrants have done spectacularly well and have amassed a great deal of wealth in a short time. They provide an economic boost for their fellow immigrants or refugees by providing employment for them. Koreans, for example, tend to hire and promote Koreans in their businesses. This is a practice, incidentally, which has come under fire from some who see this as a type of discrimination.

Third, the *professional* immigrants. These people are highly educated in professions which are in demand in the United States and which generally pay well. They are trained as doctors, physicists and engineers, to name just a few of the professions represented in this group. Their country of origin usually sees their loss as "brain drain." While they may start at the bottom of their profession in the United States, they generally move upward quickly. They tend to assimilate rapidly. As they pursue their profession in the United States, they are widely dispersed throughout the population and have little direct contact with their ethnic communities. They also tend to form relationships with fellow professionals outside their ethnic group, which soon become more important than their relationships with those from their own ethnic group who do not share their profession.

As the church ministers to today's immigrants, it needs to remember these differences. Different strategies will have to be developed to reach these three different types.

FUTURE IMMIGRATION TRENDS

Many are predicting that the numbers of immigrants will actually increase in the years to come. Today, our economy strains to the breaking point to absorb the many new immigrants who come to the United States every year. The next ten to twenty years should see a reversal of that problem. The Anglo work force is aging and many will retire in the next twenty years. As the "baby boomers" retire they will leave a large gap in the economy. The declining birth rate in the United States, especially among Anglos, means that there is no upcoming generation of Anglos to replace the boomers. Also, it has been projected that in the near future "employers will be desperate to fill jobs that many native-born don't want to do themselves. We have evolved an economy that requires people who are willing to work for very low wages in service industries—the hotel/motel sector, fruit and vegetable harvesting, and construction."[84] Because of this, it is estimated that "we will get 700,000 to 800,000 immigrants per year at the peak of our coming labor shortage from the late 1990s through 2010."[85] The ethnic community which will grow the fastest in absolute numbers is the Hispanic community, which is expected to grow by more than 11 million in the next twenty years. Asians, however, will record the largest proportionate growth. The expected takeover of Hong Kong by the Chinese Communists in 1997 may flood the western United States with an unprecedented number of Chinese. All of this means that ethnic ministry in the United States will continue to be a growing challenge in the coming decades.

The church has an enormous task ahead of her. She must learn many languages and many cultures. The work of Christ is too important to wait for the new immigrant and refugee groups to become Americanized. We must approach them on their terms and in their communities. There was a time when Germans, Swedes, Finns, Danes, and other northern European groups were new immigrant communities in the United States. Those groups have all prospered, and this country is now home to them. Now, many new strangers have appeared on our doorstep, and we have the opportunity to take them in, minister to them and welcome them to the Family of God and the grand American mosaic. May God give us the grace, the wisdom and the vision to rise above any attitudes or prejudices which would prevent us from reaching out to these new Americans. Guided by the Holy Spirit we will reach out in ministry to the many groups God has brought to our doorstep. Today as never before, the words of Jesus in Matthew 25 should ring in our ears: "Come, you who are blessed by my Father, take your inheritance, the Kingdom prepared for you since the creation of the world . . . . I was a stranger and you invited me in."

DISCUSSION QUESTIONS

1. Did your ancestors come here from another country? What do you know about their early experiences here? Did you come here from another country? What were your early experiences like?

2. There have been basically three great waves of immigration to the United States: one from northern Europe, one from southern and eastern Europe, and one from Asia, Africa, and south of the border of the United States. What is your reaction to each of these groups? What impact has each group had on this country?

3. From your reading of this chapter, what were some of the common experiences which have, over the years, motivated people to leave their native countries and come to the United States? Would those kinds of experiences have caused you to want to come to this country? What were some common experiences new immigrants had in the United States?

4. From your reading of this chapter, which groups faced unique experiences?

5.   Discuss the similarities and differences between the "older" and "newer" groups which came to this country. What impact will the differences make in your ministry to the "newer" groups?

6.   Discuss the differences between immigrants and refugees. What do these differences mean in your ministry to these two groups?

7.   What are the three types of immigrants and refugees, and what mix of these types is there in the ethnic groups in your community? How will this mix shape your ministry?

8.   If the future trends pointed out in this chapter hold true, what will this mean for the United States and for the Christian church? What challenges and opportunities do you see for the Christian church and your congregation as it reaches out to an increasingly diverse society?

2
CULTURE:
DEFINITION AND RELATED
CONCEPTS

The United States is undergoing many changes today. None is more evident or profound than the changes in the ethnic makeup of our population. The Immigration Act of 1965 opened the door to greatly increased immigration from southern Europe, Asia and Africa. Military conflicts and social strife throughout the world have brought an unprecedented number of refugees to our shores. Most of these are not of northern European extraction. The material prosperity of our country continues to attract people from all over the globe. They come hoping to make the most of the unique economic opportunities this country offers.

REACTIONS TO THE
NEW IMMIGRANTS AND REFUGEES

These newest groups of people to come to the United States have received a mixed reception. Some welcome them as a positive contribution to our nation. Others fear that the new groups of immigrants and refugees will change the United States for the worse and degrade the quality of life for us all. As Christians, we see these new Americans as people loved by God. He created them. He sent His Son, Jesus, to die for them. He earnestly desires that they all accept His offer of salvation which He, by grace, offers them.

THE BIBLICAL CONTEXT OF MINISTRY
TO IMMIGRANTS AND REFUGEES

As we reflect on the historical circumstances which have brought millions of immigrants and refugees to this country, we realize that God has had a hand in bringing them here. They did not come by accident. We believe in a God who is active in history. From beginning to end, the Bible shows God actively involved in the lives of people and in their migrations. Sometimes God causes people to migrate because of sin and sometimes in order to further His gracious plan of salvation, but He is always actively involved. As He guides the movements of individuals and groups, He also demonstrates His saving love for all nations.

God's involvement in personal and group migrations is a major Old Testament theme. In Genesis 3:23-24, God drove Adam and Eve out of the Garden of Eden because of their rebellion against Him. However, His love accompanied them as these refugees from Paradise journeyed into a thorn-choked world. In Genesis 4:13-16, Cain, after murdering Abel, migrated east of Eden and, in spite of his sin, was still protected by God. Genesis 9:18—10:32 shows how the descendants of Noah migrated from the ark and "were scattered over the earth" (Gen. 9:19). In doing so, they were fulfilling God's original intention for humans that they "be fruitful and increase in number; fill the earth and subdue it" (Gen. 1:28). In the aftermath of the Tower of Babel fiasco, God scattered people "over the face of the whole earth" (Gen. 11:9). In creating a variety of languages, God was laying the groundwork for the development of a variety of cultures on the earth.

A new chapter in God's relationship to migrants began in Genesis 12:1-3, where God called Abram to leave all that was familiar to him and migrate to a new country. From then on, Abram, whose name was later changed to Abraham, was on the move, directed and protected by God. His migrations began God's great plan to bless all nations through Jesus, a descendant of Abraham.

Jacob, in Genesis 27 and 28, deceived his father Isaac and then, to escape his brother Esau's anger, fled, but God's protecting grace followed him. He laid down to sleep in the barren wilderness and found himself at heaven's gate!

The story of Joseph in Genesis 37-50 is the story of the forced migration of a slave. Joseph was sold into slavery by his jealous brothers, taken to Egypt by slave traders, and sold to Potiphar. He was soon imprisoned, because he maintained his integrity in spite of the sexual advances of Potiphar's wife, but God was at work in all this evil. Joseph was eventually released from prison to become the second most powerful person in Egypt, and in this position was able to save his entire family from a terrible famine. At Pharaoh's invitation, Joseph's entire family, the beginning of the nation of Israel, migrated to Egypt.

The book of Exodus tells us how the Israelites grew into a nation, were made slaves by the Egyptians, and were delivered by God through the leadership of Moses. There followed forty years of migration through the wilderness until they finally entered the Promised Land. Psalm 105 recounts the migrations of God's people from Abraham to the possession of the Promised Land and praises God, whose protection and grace surrounded His people in all their travels.

The book of Ruth tells us of a young Moabite woman, Ruth, who shed her own culture, migrated to Israel, and assimilated into Jewish culture. In doing so, she became an ancestress of both David and Jesus.

The books of 1 and 2 Samuel, 1 and 2 Kings, and 1 and 2 Chronicles trace Israel's path to greatness, its tragic split into two nations, the destruction of the Northern Kingdom of Israel and the fall of the Southern Kingdom of Judah. The fall of Judah was connected with population movements. Before the fall, many Jews left the land in what is called the Diaspora and scattered to many parts of the ancient Mediterranian world. God's grace followed them wherever they went. In the aftermath of the fall, large numbers of Jews were forcibly removed from their homeland and taken into exile south of Babylon. This forced exile was God's way of purifying His people and preparing them for service. In Ezra and Nehemiah, we see God's people on the move again. They returned from their Babylonian exile to reestablish themselves in their ancestral homeland. Some, however, had become so "at home" in their new cultural surroundings that they decided not to return.

Two stories from the period of the Exile show very different ways of God's people relating to a different culture. Esther assimilated into Persian court life and in that situation was used by God to save his people from the destruction planned for them by Haman. Daniel refused to assimilate into Babylonian court life, and

God used him in that situation as a prophetic voice both to the king and the general population.

During the Exile, many Jews fell into a deep spiritual depression. In Psalm 137 they wept for their present, fondly remembered their past, and earnestly prayed for the worst to happen to their captors. Jeremiah, however, spoke a positive message of hope to them in Jeremiah 29:1-14. He advised them to "Build houses and settle down; plant gardens and eat what they produce. Marry and have sons and daughters . . . . Also, seek the peace and prosperity of the city to which I have carried you into exile. Pray to the Lord for it, because if it prospers, you too will prosper" (vss. 5-7). He affirmed that it was God's hand which had brought them into exile and it would be His hand which, after seventy years, would bring them home again. God is depicted as the Author of His people's migrations and the one who would use those migrations to accomplish His gracious plans.

The book of Jonah shows us a reluctant prophet and Jewish ethnocentrist who would rather run from God than proclaim God's message to the non-Jewish people of Nineveh. After God gave him the opportunity to think things over for three days in the belly of the fish, Jonah went to Nineveh. God's message to Nineveh through Jonah was that He intended to destroy the city because of its sins. The message produced repentance, and God, in His grace, spared the city, much to the chagrin of Jonah. The book ends with a beautiful statement of God's concern for gentile Nineveh and indeed His concern for all, regardless of their nationality.

In the New Testament, Mary made a difficult migration from Nazareth to Bethlehem before giving birth to Jesus. The journey was made necessary by a Roman decreee, but it fulfilled God's plan that His Son would be born in the city of David. Jesus and His family were soon refugees from Herod's wrath. Retracing the ancient footsteps of early Israel, the family travelled through the wilderness to Egypt and then back to Palestine. During His earthly ministry, Jesus was almost always on the move. He lived the life of a migrant, as did His disciples. When He gave the Great Commission in Matthew 28:19-20, He willed for His followers a migrant life of taking the Gospel to every nation and promised that wherever they went, He would go.

The book of Acts is the record of how the early Christian Church began fulfilling the Great Commission. On Pentecost, in Acts 2, Jews from all over the Mediterranian world had migrated to Jerusalem and were completing their celebration of Passover. It was no accident that these particular people were there on that particular day. Their migration to Jerusalem had been divinely directed. God, through the disciples, responded to this multinational gathering in a miraculous way. He enabled them to share the Gospel in the mother tongues of all the groups gathered for that celebration. Though they probably all spoke Greek as a second language, *it was God's will that they hear the Gospel in their first language.*

Acts 6 presents us with the first cross-cultural crisis of the Church. The Hellenistic Jews complained that their widows were not being properly cared for. The Church responded by choosing seven men, all Hellenistic Jews, to make sure that the problem was taken care of.

In Acts 8, a fierce persecution broke out against the Christians, and many were forced to flee as refugees throughout Judea and Samaria. Wherever they went, they shared the Gospel, and so God used their migrations for His gracious purposes. One of these Christian refugees, Philip, was used by God to bring the Gospel to an African, the Ethiopian eunuch, who was also on the move. In Acts 10:9-23, Peter, a stubborn Jewish ethnocentrist, had to be dealt with very directly by God so that he would understand that the Gospel was intended for all nations. This was necessary to prepare Peter for the opportunity to journey to Caesarea and proclaim the Gospel to Cornelius, a Roman. Following his experience with Cornelius and his family, Peter's vision of the church became multicultural (Acts 10:34-35). In Antioch, the followers of Jesus were first called Christians in connection with a mission effort directed specifically at Greeks (Acts 11:19-26). This effort was conducted by Christians who were refugees from the Jerusalem persecution.

The first Church Council (Acts 15) was convened to address the question of whether or not it was necessary to be circumcised in order to be a Christian. The broader question was how Jewish one had to be in order to be accepted as a Christian.

The Council answered that circumcision was not necessary in order to become a Christian and that salvation depended on God's grace, not Old Testament Jewish regulations. While Christian theology was binding on people of all nations, Jewish culture was not.

From Acts 13 on, the key character is Paul, the first great cross-cultural Christian missionary. His ministry provides us with the biblical model of culturally sensitive mission work. His guiding philosophy, which he summed up in 1 Corinthians 9:19-23, was to extend himself to people of other cultures, identify with them without compromising the essence of the Gospel, and strive to win as many as possible to saving faith in Jesus. Paul's ministry paved the way for Christian mission work as it moved west and north from Palestine to Europe and from there to all parts of the world.

Revelation 7:9-10 presents us with a multicultural, multinational and multilingual vision of heaven which should inspire us as we strive, under the Spirit's guidance, to reach all the cultures around us today with the Gospel. "After this I looked and there before me was a great multitude that no one could count, from every nation, tribe, people and language, standing before the throne and in front of the Lamb. They were wearing white robes and were holding palm branches in their hands. And they cried out in a loud voice: 'Salvation belongs to our God, who sits on the throne, and to the Lamb.'" The God who is active in history has brought people "from every nation, tribe, people and language" to the United States. Around us is the raw material of heaven! The challenge is to find ways to reach them so that one day they will all be a part of the heavenly choir gathered around the throne of the Lamb.

The Christian community of the United States must rise to the challenge and reach out to the many new cultures represented in our nation today. The work will be hard and—in some cases—frustrating. It will force us to reexamine the very fundamentals of our faith. It will require new philosophies of mission, new approaches in ministry, new strategies in evangelism and new programs of outreach. It will make some uncomfortable and will frighten others into a retreat to the past. Those willing to move into the future will have much learning to do. This challenge is unlike anything we've ever faced before. Even the lessons we've learned in the foreign mission field must be adjusted if they are to be helpful to us. This chapter is designed to help prepare those who seek to respond to this new God-sent opportunity to fulfill the Great Commission.

BASIC CONCEPTS AND DEFINITIONS

It is necessary to understand a number of basic concepts when ministering with people from another culture. These concepts will help us understand how to relate positively to them as unique creations of God and how to avoid the pitfalls which would make our ministry difficult and perhaps impossible. The concepts dealt with in this chapter come from the disciplines of anthropology and sociology. Some fear that introducing such concepts into the process of communicating the Gospel will lead to a relativism which will compromise the uniqueness of Christ and undermine the authority of the Bible. Before moving any further, then, I want to make two absolutely unequivocal statements. First, *Jesus Christ alone has the power to save.* Second, *the Bible is "the only rule and norm according to which all doctrines and teachers alike must be appraised and judged."*[1] The social sciences are utilized here as *servants* of the Gospel, not its master.

THE CONCEPT OF CULTURE

First, we need to understand what we mean by the concept "culture." We hear about Anglo culture, Black culture, Asian culture, Hispanic culture, and other kinds of cultures. The word "culture" is thrown around rather carelessly by many. Since we in the church want to be in ministry with people of other cultures, it is imperative that we know what we mean by the term "culture."

Culture has been defined as "the integrated system of learned patterns of behavior, ideas, and products characteristic of a society."[2] This brief definition tells us three things about culture in general. First, it is a human creation. No specific culture is biologically wired into human nature. Culture is created by thousands of decisions, insights, ideas and conjectures made by countless people over long periods of time. Second, culture is learned. The culture which was created by humans, shapes humans. From infancy each person gradually learns how to "fit in" to the surrounding society. Third, all areas of a particular culture are interrelated. We might speak of each culture having its own "ecology." Any major change in one area of a culture will cause changes throughout the culture. The second part of the definition shows how pervasive the effect of culture is on us. It shapes our behavior, how we act; our ideas, how we think (not only what we think about but also the very structure of our thinking); and our products, the physical environment with which we surround ourselves. One addition needs to be made to the above definition. Culture is dynamic. It is always in a process of change as it responds to changing circumstances.

CONSCIOUS CULTURE

Culture is made up of two parts, conscious culture and unconscious culture. Conscious culture refers to all those elements in our lives, as part of a particular culture, of which we are consciously aware and which we can define and describe. These elements express and shape how we see the world.

Our language shapes how we describe all areas of life, and different languages describe reality in different ways. A language is profoundly shaped by the culture or cultures which have developed it.

Each culture expresses a set of moral values which structures how people are to relate to each other. The value of the individual is an example of a moral value which shapes much of Anglo-American culture.

Every culture contains certain taboos, that is, activities or ideas which are absolutely forbidden. Those who break the taboos are punished, and their punishment helps strengthen the taboos and reinforces among the people of the culture a commitment to maintain those taboos. Incest, for example, is a taboo which most cultures maintain.

The art and literature of a culture express how it sees itself and the rest of the world. The art of Norman Rockwell and Andy Warhol and the writings of Thomas Jefferson and John Dewey, to name only a few, express and shape Anglo-American culture.

Rituals, "for the society as a whole, . . . offer an occasion for reaffirming its unity and expressing a sense of identity."[3] The

Fourth of July celebrations in our culture are examples of group rituals which perform these functions.

The physical products of a culture tell us much about it. Those products include its bodily adornments, toys, tools, machines, architecture, transportation systems and the physical organization of its cities. One interesting way of looking at United States culture from the point of view of physical products is to see Americans as platform builders. Our physical products show how much we value putting things up on platforms and getting them off the ground, which we consider unsanitary. The floors of our houses are platforms, as are our tables, chairs, beds, and stoves, to name but a few.

The spirituality of a culture, embodied in its religion or religions, expresses how it addresses the great questions of life and death. The Hindu belief in the transmigration of souls toward unity with Brahma is profoundly connected with the way traditional Indian culture views the purpose of life and the significance of death.

The philosophical system or systems of a culture express how it organizes the world into understandable patterns. A philosophical system which centers on the importance of the individual and his struggle for meaning expresses a culture much different from a system which centers on the importance of the group and its well-being.

Culture is also expressed in social hierachies. In traditional Vietnamese society, teachers are at the top of the social hierarchy and are highly revered and honored. Teachers are not particularly well paid, but that is unimportant because the ability to make money does not influence social position. It is a person's contribution to the well-being of the society which is of utmost importance in establishing social rank. You need only compare this with how social prominance is determined in Anglo-American culture to see how different the two cultures are.

Political patterns express a culture's understanding of life. The North American commitment to democracy and the separation of church and state are regarded by most Americans as the only enlightened way to run a country. Both of these patterns are, however, expressions of our society's belief in the importance of the individual and the subjective nature of religion. The current Iranian political pattern, which is a dictatorship of the most important religious leader in the country, is a natural outgrowth of Shi'ite Muslim culture. In Iran, the maintenance of a pure Muslim society is given more importance than the welfare of the individual, and the teachings of the Muslim faith are seen as absolute truth. These, then, are the major ingredients of what is called conscious culture. They are "conscious" because we know about them and can describe them and explain how they influence and reflect the lives of people.

UNCONSCIOUS CULTURE

Beyond conscious culture lies the realm of unconscious culture. Edward T. Hall defines unconscious culture in this way:

> The most important paradigms or rules governing behavior, the ones that control our lives, function below the level of conscious awareness and are not generally available for analysis . . . . The cultural unconscious, like Freud's unconscious, not only controls man's actions but can be understood only by painstaking processes of detailed analysis. Hence, man automatically treats what is most characteristically his own (the culture of his youth) as though it were innate.[4]

Unconscious culture therefore refers to those basic assumptions and organizing principles upon which the most profound distinctives of a culture rest but which are not understood on a conscious level even by those whose culture they shape. William Peterson notes that the concept of culture is difficult and complex because "so many institutions, rituals and practices contribute to its shaping. Its ramifications are sweeping, subtle and often unarticulated. Its effects upon us often lie below the threshold of words or even of consciousness. The culture that has shaped us shapes our way of experiencing and perceiving, of imagining and speaking, so deeply that it is very difficult to think our way outside it."[5]

The following example shows unconscious culture at work. Most Anglo-Americans show a deep concern for scheduling a time for everything and adhering to the schedule. This commitment to scheduling is considered to be the only proper, mature way to organize life. Underlying this concern, however, are a number of assumptions about time, the importance of achieving measurable results, and the importance of developing relationships, which most Anglo-Americans do not understand. These underlying assumptions are what trigger their sense of panic when something throws their schedule off by an hour and they see their carefully planned day disolving into confusion. They feel the panic and react to it but most of them cannot explain why the panic arises. Even when they intellectually understand the assumptions, they are still deeply influenced by them.

People from most of the Hispanic cultures are not deeply concerned about schedules, yet this lack of concern does not come from laziness. It comes from a set of assumptions about time, the importance of achieving measurable results and the importance of developing relationships which most of them don't understand. These assumptions are what trigger their sense of suspicion when they encounter people who seem to value clocks over people and express an offensive abruptness. Even when they understand their cultural assumptions, they are still deeply influenced by them.

Later in this chapter we will look at different sets of assumptions regarding time and the importance of measurable results and human relationships. In doing so we will learn to be sensitive to those who, in their cultural unconscious, have sets of basic assumptions about life which differ from ours.

THE PURPOSE OF CULTURE

It is obvious that the concept of culture is complex and filled with subtleties which cannot be covered in a few paragraphs. Perhaps we should ask ourselves a basic question which will help us understand this complex subject. What is the basic purpose of culture and why is it so important? The basic purpose of culture is to help us organize life in ways which are understandable and workable so that we can survive, attain our valued goals, and successfully adapt to changes in our environment.

Each culture organizes life in only one of several possible and valid ways. Because of this, culture is limiting. We cannot consider every aspect of life from every possible vantage point. To try such a thing would lead to such intellectual, emotional, and spiritual overload that we would not be able to function. Culture gives us one basic set of principles which helps us interpret life. The basic principles of our culture serve us well, even though they do limit us at certain points.

Consider the design of the eye. There is a relatively small group of cells in the center of the retina which can focus with absolute clarity. As you move away from the center the focus becomes less clear and less detailed. This design is important, because it helps us to focus our vision on whatever we are interested in at a given time without being distracted by everything else in our field of vision. If all the cells in the retina focused with the same clarity as those in the center, our brain would be so overloaded with visual signals that concentrating on a line of print in a book and reading would be very difficult if not impossible. While the design of the retina limits our vision, it also makes it possible for us to see what we want to see and to concentrate on one area without being distracted by everything else.

Culture, like the eye, lets us "see" our world from one vantage point, but in doing so it limits what we see. As we approach other cultures we regard their basic principles as both valid and limiting. It is fruitless to try to decide which culture is best, because we would do so from the vantage point of our own culture and would always end up deciding our culture was best. Rather, we should see other cultures as being other ways of looking at life and achieving the goals mentioned above. As we become aquainted with other cultures, we are given new sets of "cultural eyes" which will help us see and appreciate life in new ways. The great cultural variety around us is yet another example of human creative genius which is ours because of the image of God within us which continues to shine forth in spite of the ravages of sin.

CULTURAL RELATIVISM

This brings up the subject of cultural relativism, a subject needlessly feared by some Christians. They fear that cultural relativism will compromise the uniqueness of the Gospel and the authority of the Bible. For us as Christians, these compromises must, of course, be avoided. We believe that God's Word is authoritative truth to all people of all cultures. It is supracultural, that is, applicable to all cultures, and the standard by which all aspects of all cultures, including our own, are judged. Salvation comes through Jesus Christ alone. No other understanding of salvation, regardless of how well it relates to its surrounding culture, can be regarded as valid by Christians.

All culture is the product of fallen man and bears the marks of his glory and tragedy. All people are created in God's image, but because of sin, that image is ruined and perverted. Yet man is not an animal. In the ruins of his fallen nature, there are glimmers of God's image. Every culture will have its own unique mixture of man's fallen nature—in bondage to the devil—and the image of God—muted and in some cases almost unrecognizable. Since no culture is totally the product of God and no culture is totally the product of the devil, all cultures are relative. There are some aspects of all cultures, including our own, which we can applaud and some which we must condemn. All cultures need to hear both the Law and the Gospel. Standing on the changeless foundation of God's Word, we come to a true appreciation of the relative presence of good and evil, sin and grace, God and Satan in all cultures.

One final word of caution concerning culture: when we talk about a culture which influences millions of people, we are necessarily reduced to generalities. Within every major culture there are many sub-groups, each of which has experienced the culture in different ways. Social status, ecomonic conditions, occupation or profession, political beliefs, social environment (rural, small town, urban), family environment, family history, personal experiences, and a host of other variables, influence the way general cultural principles affect individuals and the many sub-groups which make up a culture. We can make certain broad statements, for example, about Anglo-American culture, but that doesn't mean that, having understood those principles, we now know what makes every Anglo-American tick. There are significant differences between an Anglo-American with a rural midwestern, Germanic, farming background and one with an urban, northeastern, English, professional class background. When we move into a new culture we always come as learners, who, having learned the general principles of the culture, have the patience and sensitivity to catch the subtleties of its sub-groups and the ultimate uniqueness of each of its members.

THE DEFINITION OF AN ETHNIC GROUP

What constitutes an "ethnic group"? There is a problem with terminology that becomes evident when we refer to the present challenge in the United States today of reaching new groups with the Gospel. Sometimes this is called "ethnic ministry" and sometimes "cross-cultural ministry." Sometimes we refer to "ethnic groups," "cultural groups," "minority groups," "racial groups," or "nationalities" when refering to the new groups in the United

States which we are trying to reach with the Gospel. The term which will be used most in this book is "ethnic group" or simply "ethnics."

The terms used are not as important as what they mean. There is the danger that our terminology may become so imprecise and clouded that we will fail to define clearly the scope of each group we seek to reach. If we do not have a clear understanding of the boundaries of various ethnic groups, we will have great difficulty preparing ethnic ministry resources and establishing ethnic ministry goals.

It seems useful to consider five factors when establishing the boundaries of an ethnic group. *Race* is one factor. By race we mean that a group of people belongs to one of the major racial groups of the human family. Racial groups are usually defined by uniqueness in skin color and one or more distinct physical characteristics. This does not ignore the fact that racial groups today tend to be "soft on the edges," with many people, owing to inter-racial marriage, being able to claim membership in two or more races. Also noted is the fact that some cultures, such as many of the Hispanic cultures, embrace people from a variety of racial groups. We should be careful to remember that skin color is a purely surface way of differentiating between large groups of people and has no impact, in and of itself, on how people think or act or what they can accomplish. Each race has produced many profoundly beautiful, insightful and unique cultures. *Region* is another factor. By region we mean that geographical area which has traditionally been the home of a group, regardless of where part or most of that group now lives. Many times region refers to the same area as nationality but not always. Certain peoples have lived in the same region for centuries, during which there have been many redrawings of national boundaries. *Culture* is a third factor and is here defined in the same way as it was in the section above. *Language*, though a part of culture, is also thought of as a separate factor when defining an ethnic group. *Religion*, also a part of culture, is yet another factor in defining the limits of an ethnic group.

Because of the many variables present in every culture and the uniqueness of each individual, any definition of ethnicity will become somewhat ill-fitting in certain circumstances. Realizing its limitations, we will use the definition of an ethnic group as a group of people who share a common racial, regional, cultural, linguistic, and religious background.

ETHNOCENTRISM, PREJUDICE, RACISM, AND PATERNALISM

Cross-cultural relationships on both the individual and group levels can take a number of different shapes. The possibilities range from natural human ethnocentrism to prejudice, racism, and paternalism.

Ethnocentrism is the feeling on the part of an individual that his group is the center of the world and the best in the world, and therefore he must be more concerned with it than with any other group. This group might be his nation, his ethnic group, or his school, but whatever it is, he sees its needs as being centrally important and ultimately good. Ethnocentrism seems to be an outgrowth of our natural inclination toward pride and self-centeredness which infects us all because of the Fall. Because of our sinful nature, each of us tends to believe that we are the center of the universe and that our own needs are more important than the needs of others. The Christian faith seeks to soften our self-centeredness and redeem our pride so that we can truly be concerned for the needs of others to the point of self-sacrifice, but for a variety of reasons this process is difficult and remains incomplete. Ethnocentrism is, therefore, an expression of proud self-centeredness. It does not so much look down on other groups as elevate the importance of its own group. Comedian Mel Brooks, in his thousand-year-old man routine, informs his audience that the first national anthem in history was "Cave nine is the best cave in the world." That's a perfect expression of ethnocentrism.

Prejudice goes a step further than ethnocentrism. It projects negative attitudes and feelings toward all other groups except its own. Thus, students at one high school tend to indulge in a great deal of prejudice as they prepare for the "big game" against a rival school. By game time, many of the most rabid fans have convinced themselves that the game is their opportunity to expose the inferiority of the other school. In most cases, prejudice is expressed toward a group that differs from "our" group. The reason much prejudice has racial overtones is that race is a very obvious point at which some groups differ from others. Prejudice develops as ethnocentrism and moves from an attitude which elevates the importance of "our" group to an attitude which belittles the importance and finally the humanity of "their" group. We prejudge them in a negative way because we have prejudged ourselves in a positive way.

Racism moves a step further and opens the most destructive possibilities in interpersonal and intergroup relationships. It actively seeks ways to humiliate, dominate, and control those who are the objects of prejudice. The most vicious part of racism is that, many times, it expresses hatred toward others based on God-given qualities such as skin color, physical characteristics and national origin. There are also times—and the Jewish people have experienced this repeatedly—when people have been subjected to racism because of their religion. Racism, left unchecked, can lead to social, emotional, and legal oppression and to the suspension of civil liberties (as in the policies of Apartheid in South Africa), to imprisonment (as with the Japanese in California during World War II), to occasional lynchings (as with Blacks in the south until recently), and ultimately to attempted genocide (as with the Jews in Nazi Germany).

One further term needs to be addressed: paternalism. *Paternalism* is simply an outwardly polite form of racism. It hides its disregard for the humanity of others in a velvet glove and dresses it up in a Sunday suit. Its goals are the same as outwardly ugly racism. It simply seeks to use more subtle methods.

This presents a challenge to the church. The open ugliness of racism is seldom seen in American Christianity, but widespread paternalism persists. Being kind with paternalism only assures that its tragedy will continue. The church needs to face paternalism, see beyond its mask, and find ways, through the power of the Gospel, to purge this poison from the Body of Christ. When we approach another group with the Gospel, if there is paternalism in our hearts, they will feel its evil even if we are not aware of it, and it will drown out our message. Paternalism is a major enemy of the Great Commission as the church seeks to be fruitful in cross-cultural ministry.

An example of the necessity of facing up to the negative feelings we have about other ethnic groups comes from the ministry of the famous missionary Frank C. Laubach. In 1929, he was given a mission opportunity he had been praying for since he first arrived in the Philippines in 1915. He was sent to the island of Mindanao to begin mission work among the Maranaws, a fiercely independent group of Muslims who had deep anti-Christian feelings. He left his wife and young son in Manila where they would be safe and moved into a small house on a military reservation near Signal Hill. He began his work with great eagerness but experienced frustration after frustration. He, along with his dog, Tip, would climb Signal Hill every evening at sunset, and there Laubach would spend time in prayer. One evening on Signal Hill, he had a life-changing spiritual experience. He described it this way:

> One evening I was sitting on Signal Hill looking over the province that had me beaten. Tip had his nose up under my arm trying to lick the tears off my cheeks. My lips began to move and it seemed to me that God was speaking. "My Child" my lips said, "you have failed because you do not really love these Maranaws. You feel superior to them because you are white. If you can forget you are an American and think only how I love them, they will respond." I answered back to the sunset, "God, I don't know whether You spoke to me through my lips, but if You did, it was the truth. I hate myself. My plans have all gone to pieces. Drive me out of myself and come and take possession of me and think Thy thoughts in my mind." In that terrible, wonderful hour on Signal Hill I became color-blind. Ever since, I have been partial to tan, the more tan the better! Every missionary goes through some such experience as that—or comes home defeated. After that night on Signal Hill when God killed my racial prejudice and made me color-blind, it seemed as though He worked miracles at every turn.[6]

Laubach's experience applies to us as we seek to minister together with people from the many ethnic groups in the United States today. While we might well prefer the concept of color-appreciative to color-blindness, still, Laubach's experiences and reflections are valuable. We *must* face up to whatever prejudice, paternalism or racism we carry within us, ask for His forgiveness and let Him give us the power to love the people of other cultures the way He loves them. This must happen or we will surely fail our Lord in the important task of cross-cultural ministry in the United States.

To sum up, we all have a certain amount of ethnocentrism, that is, self-centered pride, in us owing to our fallen humanity. This pride tends to rob us of our enthusiasm for reaching other groups with the Gospel. Because of ethnocentrism, we will be constantly tempted to spend more

energy on creating a church in which we and "our kind" feel
comfortable than on creating a church which can reach out to
other ethnic groups. Prejudice is carried about by many of us.
It may not do social harm to the group against which we are
prejudiced, but it will poison our own souls. For a Christian,
a soul poisoned by prejudice is a terrible liability when it
comes to sharing the Gospel. As Frank Laubach discovered,
prejudice cripples even our best human efforts to fulfill the
Great Commission. Racism is capable of the worst imaginable
crimes against humanity, and it arises when prejudice is
allowed to grow unchecked. Paternalism is subtle racism and,
when pressed, is capable of as much evil as racism. Any
church which allows a place for racism or paternalism not
only destroys its capacity for fulfilling the Great Commission
but also embraces the instrument of its own death as a part of
the Body of Christ.

Having identified these foes of cross-cultural ministry,
let us have the courage to confess where we have tolerated
them, claim God's forgiveness for the damage they have done
to our ministry in the past, and utilize the power of the Spirit
in a never-ending war against them.

CULTURAL PROJECTION

Another threat to cross-cultural ministry is cultural
projection. Cultural projection happens when the rules of one
culture are used to interpret the words, attitudes, and actions
of people from a different culture. Each culture has its own
rules and guiding principles which explain why people act the
way they do. For example, Anglo-American culture values
being on time and keeping on schedule—even when it means
cutting short a satisfying encounter with someone. "I'm late;
I have to go" is a statement which, in our[7] culture, generally
gives blanket permission to end one appointment or event and
go on to the next. If we are late, we apologize. The later we
are, the more profusely we apologize. On the other hand,

Vietnamese culture values quality human contacts and pursuing an encounter through to its logical conclusion even if that means being late for another commitment. Being late for appointments is not regarded as a social problem. Therefore, apologies are not generally offered for tardiness. This kind of difference between cultures, combined with cultural projection, can lead to very unpleasant experiences.

If an Anglo-American[8] who does not understand Vietnamese culture makes an appointment with a Vietnamese-American who does not understand Anglo-American culture, a negative experience is likely to happen. The Anglo-American, true to his culture, will arrive a few minutes early. The Vietnamese-American may arrive half an hour late and never apologize for his lateness. The Anglo-American may well make a negative judgment about the Vietnamese-American and even make negative comments to him. These will be based on the Anglo-American concern for being on time and his judgment that lack of timeliness indicates lack of respect for him and lack of maturity on the part of the one who is late. The Vietnamese-American may respond to this by assuming that the Anglo-American, because of his lack of politeness, his mania for schedules, and his disinterest in quality social contacts unfettered by time concerns, is cold and shallow. This is cultural projection at work. Both people in the example were acting appropriately according to their culture. Each used the rules of his culture to make inappropriate judgments about the words and actions of the other.

Before we can accurately evaluate the behavior of someone in another culture we must understand the rules which govern behavior in that culture. If we do not do the work necessary to achieve this understanding, we will blindly stagger from one negative experience to another as we attempt to relate across cultural lines. This will cause us much personal pain and will make cross-cultural ministry a nightmare. Acquiring this understanding takes time and effort but will ultimately lead to deep and rewarding relationships with people from another culture. Once these relationships develop, successful cross-cultural ministry is possible.

LOW CONTEXT AND HIGH CONTEXT CULTURES[9]

As we reach out with the Gospel to people in cultures other than our own we need to understand the difference between a low context culture and a high context culture. "Context" refers to the amount and intensity of interpersonal relationships deemed necessary by a given culture in order to communicate, do business, build trust, or make a decision. It answers the question, "How long do we need to know each other and how many shared experiences do we need to have before we can work together in a beneficial way?" Context is roughly equivalent to Christian fellowship in intra- or inter-church relationships.

Low context and high context are not static terms but represent two extremes of a continuum. Some cultures, such as Swiss and Scandinavian, are very low context cultures. Their cultures function with a marginal emphasis on interpersonal relationships. Swiss businessmen can do business with each other in a very efficient way while feeling no inclination to know each other as human beings. Other cultures, such as German and Anglo-American, are a little higher on the context continuum. There is some need to know and relate to others in order to do business but personal relationships, outside of family and close friends, tend to be shallow and temporary. Still other cultures, such as Hispanic, Asian, and Black, are high context cultures which place a high value on interpersonal relationships, and, indeed, without a considerable amount of "getting to know" another person, they will be reluctant to communicate, do business, extend trust, or make decisions. It is important to understand where a particular culture fits on the context continuum in order to understand what is needed to enter into significant ministry with them.

MONOCHRONIC AND POLYCHRONIC TIME[10]

Every culture has developed a way of viewing time. "Monochronic time" and "polychronic time" are terms which describe the two major ways of viewing time, and they are quite different from each other. A culture's way of viewing time will deeply affect its entire fabric. Edward T. Hall, in his book *Beyond Culture*, compares monochronic time and polychronic time in these words:

> Monochronic time (M-time) and polychronic time (P-time) represent two variant solutions to the use of both time and space as organizing frames for activities. Space is included because the two systems (time and space) are functionally interrelated. M-time emphasizes schedules, segmentation, and promptness. P-time systems are characterized by several things happening at once. They stress involvement of people and completion of transactions rather than adherence to preset schedules. P-time is treated as much less tangible than M-time. P-time is apt to be considered a point rather than a ribbon or a road, and that point is sacred.[11]

Hall continues:

> Particularly distressing to Americans is the way in which appointments are handled by polychronic people. Appointments just don't carry the same weight as they do in the United States. Things are constantly shifted around. Nothing seems solid or firm, particularly plans for the future, and there are always changes in the most important plans right up to the very last minute . . . .
> For M-time people reared in the northern European tradition, time is linear and segmented like a road or a ribbon extended forward into the future and backward to the past. It is also tangible; they speak of it as being saved, spent, wasted, lost, made up, accelerated, slowed down, crawling, and running out . . . . It should be mentioned that without schedules and something very

much like the M-time system, it is doubtful if our
industrial civilization could have developed as it has.[12]

Monochronic and polychronic time, for all their
differences, are not mutually exclusive. They are, in fact,
interrelated as two poles on a continuum, much like the low
context—high context continuum. All cultures are concerned
with both time and events. Some, such as Anglo-American,
are very concerned with the precise moment things begin and
end, while others, such as most Hispanic cultures, are
concerned with the day of an event, and even, to some
degree, with the hour of an event, but a few minutes one way
or the other is of little consequence. Some cultures, such as
most Hispanic cultures, while they are extremely concerned
about the quality of events, also are aware of time and apply
their understanding of time to their conduct of events. Other
cultures, such as Anglo-American, while they are extremely
concerned about time, also pay attention to the quality of an
event. Time-oriented people expect that if they are going to
spend their valuable time at an event, it had better be good!

Beyond the interrelationship between time concerns
and event concerns, there are other ways in which those
toward the time-oriented end of the continuum differ from
those toward the event-oriented end of the continuum. Time-
oriented people carefully plan the schedule of an event to
make maximum use of the time alloted to it, while event-
oriented people "will bring people together without planning
a detailed schedule and see what develops."[13] Time-oriented
people will make long, middle and short range plans for the
future, while event-oriented people tend to live in the here
and now with only minimal plans or concerns about the
future. Time-oriented people will equate time with money
and/or production, while event-oriented people will equate
time with relationships and trust. There are, obviously, many
pitfalls nearby when time-oriented and event-oriented people
attempt a cooperative venture. Being sensitive to the very

different ways in which different cultures view time will help us avoid those pitfalls.

These, then, are some of the concepts and terms we need to understand as we lay the groundwork for fruitful cross-cultural ministry today. Later in this book, we will see how these concepts can help shape a successful strategy for reaching the many cultures represented in the United States today. Before doing that, we will take a brief look at the American historical context of the unity-diversity debate. It will give us a fruitful context in which to consider that same question within the Christian Church.

DISCUSSION QUESTIONS

1. Discuss God's grace and judgment as they relate to the various migrations of individuals and groups which are recorded in the Bible. Do you believe God is still in control of today's people migrations? What impact does this have on your attitudes toward those who have migrated to our country?

2. Discuss the vision of heaven which is presented in Revelation 7:9-10 and how it applies to the church's ministry in our diverse society.

3. Define and discuss: culture, conscious culture, unconscious culture, and the purpose of culture.

4. What is the relationship between cultural relativism and the Gospel?

5. How did this chapter define an ethnic group? Using that definition, name the ethnic groups in your community.

6.   Discuss your thoughts and feelings regarding ethnocentrism, prejudice, racism, and paternalism. To what degree do you, your congregation, and your denomination currently reflect any of these attitudes? Have you ever been on the receiving end of any of these attitudes? What was that like?

7.   Give some examples of cultural projection. Have you ever been involved in cultural projection, either as the one judging or as the one being judged? How do you feel about that experience?

8.   In your understanding of relationships, are you low context or high context? In your understanding of time, are you monochronic or polychronic? Have you had contacts with people who viewed relationships and time in a way which was much different from the way you viewed them? What was that like?

3

ETHNICITY IN THE UNITED STATES— A HISTORICAL SKETCH
THE ROOTS OF THE UNITY-DIVERSITY DEBATE

Following the success of the Revolutionary War, the former Colonies faced many questions concerning nationhood. Chief among these was what would be the design and structure of their government. All were committed to democracy, but there were fundamental differences among them regarding how much the government should control the affairs of the former colonies and the lives of their citizens. New York, Rhode Island, Pennsylvania, and Maryland opted for religious and cultural pluralism, where government made little or no intrusion into the affairs of its citizenry. On the other hand, Massachusetts, Connecticut, and Virginia opted for a decidedly nonpluralistic design. Influenced by Protestantism, they sought to create a new and unified citizenry, leaving diverse histories and cultural traits behind to form a single civic culture.

When representatives of these two viewpoints met to create a governmental structure for the new nation, the nonpluralist and pluralist points of view collided. The nonpluralists, or centrists as they were called, were represented by such men as Alexander Hamilton and James Madison. They argued for a strong central government which would shape all the states into a unified nation. They foresaw a nation where the patterns of life would be the same everywhere. The laws and traditions established by central government would become the laws and traditions of all the states. They valued unity above all. The pluralists, or localists as they were called, were represented by such men as Thomas Jefferson and Sam Adams. They argued for a weak central government with major power residing in the state and local governments. They wanted each state to be able to establish laws and traditions free from outside interference. They foresaw a nation in which each state would develop its own unique fabric of life. They valued diversity above all.

The Articles of Confederation, which was the first document to shape the American government, was strongly weighted toward the localist philosophy. The weak central government it created was ineffective in resolving even simple disputes among the various states. It soon became evident that some changes would have to be made.

In the summer of 1787, the Constitutional Convention met in Philadelphia to consider what changes were needed. Upon their arrival at the convention, most of the delegates assumed that all they had gathered to do was to fine-tune the Articles of Confederation. What emerged from the meeting, however, was a whole new document, our present Constitution, which gave increased power to the central government. Being sensitive to the concerns of the localists, the delegates were careful not to make it a one-sided document. It still gave significant powers to the states in many areas. Because of this, the Constitution did not resolve the question of central control versus local control. Instead, it kept them in tension, and certain portions of the Constitution, depending one one's political philosophy, can be interpreted either as giving more or less power to the states in important areas.

The Constitution did not, therefore, resolve the question of unity and diversity in this country. The bloodiest war in our history, the Civil War, was fought over the question of how much right the states have to control the lives of their citizens without interference from the federal government. While the immediate social issue was slavery, the underlying philosophical issue was the central government's power versus states' rights, or unity versus diversity. Not even the Civil War laid that issue to rest. It still surfaces from time to time. It underlies much of the debate which swirls around various nominees for the Supreme Court, since that is the body which has the ongoing responsibility of interpreting the

Constitution and its careful balancing of central government and local government powers.

UNITY, DIVERSITY, AND THE QUESTION OF CITIZENSHIP

Another important question for the fledgling nation was, what does it mean to be an American? Since most of its citizens were foreign born, this question raised two more questions. First, how much of my former cultural and national identity, that is, my ethnicity, may I keep and still be considered an American? Second, what new ideas, behaviors, allegiances, and skills do I need to adopt before I can be considered an American? To put these questions another way, one could ask how much unlike others may I be, or, how much like others must I be? Yet another way of expressing this dilemma is, how much diversity will be allowed and how much unity will be required among the many ethnic groups within the United States? Thus, the question of ethnicity and one's identity as an American presents the same basic poles of tension as the ongoing debate over the central government's power to enforce unity and the states' rights to maintain their diversity.

THE ROOTS OF PLURALISM

From the beginning of United States history, there have been two schools of thought regarding those who immigrate to this country. Some, echoing the political traditions of Rhode Island and Pennsylvania, championed a pluralism which gave all people the right to be who they wanted to be. The young nation was proud of the many different groups which had found a new home in the United States and pointed to this diversity as mark of its uniqueness. The Constitution was structured to give all groups the right, within certain broad limitations, to establish their unique identities without the fear of being labeled "un-American". This constitutional protection of ethnicity simply recognized a longstanding reality. From early in the colonial period, diversity was a fact of life in the New World. In 1643, the French missionary Isaac Jogues reported hearing eighteen[1] different languages being spoken in New Amsterdam alone. It must be stated, however, that those who celebrated diversity celebrated *European* diversity. Blacks were not considered citizens, and Native

Americans were seen mainly as savages who deserved to be exterminated.

Early in American history, it was easy to be pluralistic. The frontier offered any group which felt stifled by others the opportunity to push further west. There, in the isolation of the boundless land, it could express its unique lifestyle in an environment which would neither affect nor upset others. A classic expression of this pluralistic idea is a line from Emma Lazarus' poem on the base of the Statue of Liberty: "Give me your tired, your poor, Your huddled masses yearning to breath free."[2] European monarchies might have oppressed the people and forced them to live in whatever way the royal power structure demanded, but it was different in America. Here, so the poem seems to be saying, you can be whatever you want to be. Here diversity is not only tolerated, it is celebrated.

THE ROOTS OF NONPLURALISM

A second school of thought regarding ethnicity and American identity traces its origins back to the political traditions of Massachusetts and Connecticut, which were nonpluralistic. From the beginning of American history there was the belief that a "new man" was being created in the New World—one who would shed all his past allegiances and fit into a new, ideal mold. He would, in other words, assimilate. The Declaration of Independence gave eloquent voice to the nonpluralists desire to create both a "new man" and a "virtuous republic" which would become the high point of human civilization.

This nonpluralist, or assimilationist, dream of the new man being created on the American continent was described in 1782 by the French-born writer J. Hector St. John de Crevecoeur in this classic passage from his *Letters from an American Farmer*. "I could point out to you a family . . . whose grandfather was an Englishman, whose wife was Dutch, whose son married a French woman, and whose present four sons have now four wives of different nations. **He** is an American, who, leaving behind him all his ancient prejudices and manners, receives new ones from the new mode of life he has embraced . . . . Here individuals of all nations are melted into a new race of men."[3]

Those who did not easily and quickly "melt" were seen as threats to the nation. Benjamin Franklin, an ardent assimilationist, worried that the Germans would ruin Pennsylvania:

"This will in a few years become a German Colony: Instead of their Learning our Language, we must learn theirs, or live as in a foreign country. Already the English begin to quit particular Neighborhoods surrounded by Dutch, being made uneasy by the Disagreeableness of dissonant Manners; and in Time, Numbers will probably quit the Province for the same Reason. Besides, the Dutch under-live, and are thereby enabled to under-work and under-sell the English; who are thereby extremely incommoded, and consequently disgusted, so that there can be no cordial Affection or Unity between the two Nations.'"[4]

Even Thomas Jefferson, who believed in pluralism and encouraged diversity, worried that European immigrants would overwhelm the English presence in the new nation and change its character for the worse. The message of the assimilationists was that in America all ethnic differences must fade away so that a new race of people, unpolluted by the national rivalries and undemocratic ideas of Europe, might show the world the way to utopia. The pressure to assimilate was especially intense in the cities. There the many ethnic groups daily encountered one another, and their differences were the cause of much friction. It seemed to many that assimilation was necessary for social harmony.

It was against the backdrop of these two competing versions of American life that the new nation struggled to establish some kind of standards for accepting people as citizens. Despite all the debate over pluralism and assimilation and the fear that certain ethnic groups were harming the country by not assimilating, the United States declined to define citizenship in ethnic, religious or linguistic terms. America and the United States—the two names by which the nation identitifed itself to the world—were both non-ethnic in nature. Its principle of the separation of church and state meant that American identity would not be connected to a particular religion. Even though in the minds of most Americans being American and being Protestant were closely identified, this idea never received governmental sanction. While English was the language of the land, no official attempt was made to suppress other languages as though they were un-American.

THE ESSENTIALS OF AMERICAN IDENTITY

What, then, was necessary before a person could be an American citizen? The answer was simple. All a person had to do was commit himself to the abstract principles of liberty, equality, and democracy. This new nation was determined to define itself "by its ideals, rather than by ethnicity."[5] This decision was consistent with the birth of the nation. The American Revolution was not fought over ethnic, racial or national origin issues. It was fought over the ideological issues of liberty, equality, and democracy. These three ideas formed the basis of the Declaration of Independence and the Constitution and so were seen as an adequate standard for admitting people as citizens. The debate over ethnicity and the relative merits and demerits of certain groups of immigrants would ebb and flow over the years. Racism would rear its ugly head and oppress certain groups. Too often, this racism would be incorporated into the legal framework of the nation. Through it all, however, the nation officially rejected the idea that a person's country of origin automatically precluded him from being an American. Ethnic differences could be tolerated and even celebrated since almost everyone assumed that commitment to the uniquely American ideals of liberty, equality, and democracy would soon create an entirely new race of people with its own unique ethnicity.

IMMIGRATION AND ETHNIC ISSUES FROM 1790 TO 1880

The immigration laws which were passed in the 1790s show that the debate over how to accept immigrants as citizens was still very volatile. The immigration law of 1790 provided for only a two-year wait before any free white person was allowed to become a citizen. Some protested that the two-year wait was too long. The naturalization law of 1795 specified that a person was required to renounce any hereditary title before becoming a citizen and extended the waiting period to five years. Because of the French revolution and the fears that the passions which were tearing Europe apart might be imported to the United States, the naturalization law of 1798 required a fourteen year wait for citizenship. This policy did not last long. In 1802, with the full support of President Jefferson, the waiting period was reduced to five years again. These changes in waiting periods reflect the ongoing debate concerning how much diversity the United States could tolerate. As the toleration of diversity decreased, the waiting period increased and vice versa.

Until after the Civil War, immigration was controlled by the state governments. The federal government didn't even keep statistics on immigration until 1820, and even then its statistics were rather slipshod. Even though the federal government exercised its constitutional right to grant or refuse to grant citizenship, it took no real interest in regulating who took up residence within its borders. It was not until the 1880s that immigration was placed under the exclusive control of the federal government. By that time the first great wave of immigrants had already arrived in the United States.

THE CATHOLIC CONTROVERSY

The first great ethnic controversy centered on religion, not country of origin. There had been Roman Catholics in this country since long before the Revolution, but their numbers had been small. From the beginning, however, they had aroused the suspicion of many. In 1700, a Massachussetts law demanded the expulsion from the colony of "all and every Jesuit, seminary priest, missionary, or other spiritual or ecclesiastical person made or ordained by . . . the pope or See of Rome"[6] by November 10 of that year. Some feared that the hierarchical government of the Catholic church caused Catholics to harbor undemocratic and hence un-American ideas. Others were suspicious of Catholics because their worship service was conducted in Latin. For most people, however, the small Catholic communities in the United States aroused no particular panic.

In the mid 1800s, things changed. Between 1830 and 1850, large numbers of Catholic immigrants flooded into the United States. Some were from Germany, but most were from Ireland. Catholics numbered about 35,000 in 1790. In 1850, there were 1.6 million, and by 1860, that number had increased to 3.1 million.[7] This enormous influx "made the Roman Catholic Church the largest denominational body in the United States."[8] Many had always assumed that being Protestant and being American went hand in hand. The flood of Catholic immigrants challenged that idea. To make the situation even more tense the 1830s saw a tremendous religious revival among conservative Protestants. The leaders of this revival were strongly anti-Catholic and equated the Pope and the Catholic church with the Antichrist and his followers. Their conclusion was that you couldn't be a good Catholic and a good American at the same time. Irish Catholic immigrants were often cited as proof of this. The Irish were having difficulties fitting into American society, and this was seen as having more to do with their religion than their country of origin.

Another cause for distrust of Catholics was their school system. It was almost an article of faith in the 1800s that the public school system, to which everyone went, was a necessary part of transforming immigrants into genuine Protestant Americans. The separate Catholic school system was regarded as a way of preserving religious error and undemocratic ideas. The Catholics' opposition to the King James Version of the Bible and their efforts to receive public funds to support Catholic schools so inflamed passions that there were anti-Catholic riots in Philadelphia in 1844.

Anti-Catholic passions also fueled the rise of the American Party, also known as the "Know Nothings". Its rise to power was meteoric. "By the fall of 1854, it had elected seventy-five persons to Congress."[9] Its fall from power was just as meteoric. By the outbreak of the Civil War its political power had collapsed, but its fundamental ideas lived on. Its strident brand of patriotism, its vision of a fundamentalist Protestant America and its mistrust of any kind of religious, linguistic, or cultural diversity would surface again.

Because of anti-Catholicism, any immigrant group which was mainly Catholic was automatically suspect. Where ethnicity and Catholicism seemed to go hand in hand, as with the Irish, ethnicity, for the first time in the history of this country, was seen as un-American. It would take a long time before many Protestant Americans could regard Catholics as real Americans. By the time of the Civil War, however, the worst of the anti-Catholic episodes was over.

During the Civil War, many immigrants served with distinction in the Union Army, and this helped reduce the suspicion that the various immigrant groups had a low level of loyalty to the United States. The fledgling Republican party strongly supported laws which encouraged immigration. After the Civil War there was great economic expansion, and immigrants were welcomed to fill the country's growing labor needs. In Europe, recruiters representing various states, territories, and corporations, swarmed over the countryside inviting people to come and share in the boundless wealth and opportunity of the United States. All were assured that they would find complete acceptance. The recruiters were spectacularly successful. In the twenty years following the Civil War, millions came to the United States searching for a better life. Much of the world was beginning to see the United States as a golden land where all could prosper. In the midst of the post-war expansion and prosperity, questions regarding ethnicity caused little public debate and expressions of ethnicity caused little public concern.

1880 TO 1900
RISING CONCERNS OVER THE NEW IMMIGRANTS

At first all were welcome, for the upswing. in immigrants came mostly from northern Europe. The various northern European ethnic groups had been represented for generations in the United States. All assumed that these new immigrants would fit into American life just as well as their earlier countrymen had. In the 1880s and 1890s, however, a trend developed which caused concern and even panic.

In the east, concerns were voiced over the upswing of immigration from southern Europe. Southern Europeans such as Jews, Slavs, Poles, Serbs and Italians, were considered by many to be "innately inferior and racially unassimilable. Popular journals were filled with hostile references to the newcomers."[10] Rather than settling in isolated rural areas, these immigrants flooded into the cities and were highly visible. They were mostly poor, uneducated, and unskilled and came with little understanding of American life. Wrapped in the comfort of their large urban communities, they appeared to have no interest in learning English and assimilating into mainstream American culture. Many native-born Americans feared that these strange new ethnics would overwhelm the United States. Rather than the southern Europeans becoming Americanized, there was a deep fear that this country would become like southern Europe, and the unique qualities of American life would be destroyed forever.

The west was in a panic over Chinese immigration. The Chinese, since they were both non-white and non-Christian, were considered doubly unassimilable. The Chinese Exclusion Act of 1882 sought to stop the flow of Chinese once and for all so they they could not overwhelm the country. The continual harassment of the Chinese was one expression of the fear that they endangered the quality of life for all Americans. The rationale seemed to be that since they could not be assimilated they must be eliminated.

For the first time in the history of the United States, the country began to believe that it must exclude or severely limit certain ethnic groups in order to preserve its national identity. But even then there was no headlong rush to define the United States in ethnic terms. The groups which were held in suspicion were not so regarded only because of their ethnicity. It was widely believed that certain ethnic groups could never fully understand or give their loyalty to the basic American principles of liberty, equality, and democracy. Much of the bias against southern Europeans and Asians was caused by the belief that these groups could never embrace the ideological foundation of American identity.

1900 THROUGH THE END OF WORLD WAR II
THE MELTING POT

The first quarter of the twentieth century saw an increase in the controversy surrounding ethnicity. In 1909, Israel Zangwill's play *The Melting Pot* began a long run in New York City. The concept of the United States as a melting pot in which all ethnic differences disappeared and a new American identity was forged, was not new. Because of the great popularity of Zangwill's play, however, it became the major way of explaining the relationship of ethnicity to American identity. The melting pot ideal was that ethnic consciousness was a transitory stage through which immigrants passed on their way to becoming full-fledged

Americans. The result of this was that many began seeing any persistant ethnic consciousness as being un-American. At the very least, it was seen as a barrier which prevented the United States from achieving its age old dream of creating a "new man" and a "virtuous republic."

There was much ethnic consciousness in this country at the beginning of the twentieth century. There were millions of recent immigrants who had no real interest in abandoning their ethnic identity. This massive, ethnically conscious, immigrant population caused a deep and increasing uneasiness among native-born Americans. The uneasiness had to do with more than ethnic concerns. At the beginning of the twentieth century there were a number of radical political and social theories gaining popularity in Europe. There was great fear that many of these new immigrants were devotees of these theories and that they intended to overthrow the United States government and destroy democracy. By the eve of World War I, many Americans already believed that Bolshevism, later to be called Communism, posed a significant threat to the country.

WORLD WAR I AND ETHNICITY

World War I exploded at a bad time for immigrant communities in the United States. Many immigrants found that they had to make the hard choice between staying in this country or going home and joining the war effort in their native countries. Many decided to return to their homelands, and this came as a shock to many native-born Americans. Many soon began to regard all ethnically conscious immigrants as enemies within. Suspicion and anger was centered on the large German-American community.

The German-American community was still tightly knit. German language newspapers and periodicals abounded. Both the German Catholics and German Lutherans had their own separate school systems. The German Lutherans often conducted both their schools and their church services in German and, as a result, were held in deep suspicion. Many believed that the German-American community was preparing to give aid to a German invasion of the United States. A statement by Theodore Roosevelt summed up the way many English-speaking Americans felt. "The men of German blood who have tried to be both Germans and Americans are no Americans at all, but traitors to America and tools and servants of Germany against America . . . . Hereafter we must see that the melting pot really does . . . melt. There should be but one language in this country—the English."[11] Most Germans shed their language and hid their culture to avoid further suspicion and hostility. In a farmhouse in southern Indiana, my grandfather brought his family together and announced that henceforth they would speak only English.

THE AMERICANIZATION MOVEMENT

World War I was not just a problem for German-Americans. It was a problem for all immigrant communities. The War created tremendous pressure to abandon ethnicity and melt completely into general American culture. Americanization, as it was called, sought to reduce ethnic consciousness to nothing more than a remembrance of ethnic origins. Americanization, as a movement, had begun around 1900. In 1919, Emory S. Bogardus, in his book *Essentials of Americanization*, stated that "Americanization is a phase of assimilation—a process which transforms unlike attitudes and behavior into like attitudes and behaviors."[12] He further defined Americanization in the following five statements:

> Americanization is teaching foreigners to be satisfied
> with their jobs. Americanization is the suppression by
> vigorous means of all radical elements in our country.
> Americanization is the reducing of the foreign-born to a
> uniformity of opinions and beliefs in harmony with
> Americanism. Americanization means teaching English
> and civics to foreigners in order to enable them to

> secure naturalization papers. Americanization is a
> paternalistic program for helping ignorant foreigners by
> utilizing the superior ability of the native-born.[13]

In the first phase of its existence it sought to use the schools as an Americanizing instrument. Some in public education accepted this concept with great zeal, while others, such as John Dewey, sought to soften its bias against ethnic consciousness.

With the outbreak of World War I, the Americanization movement became much more strident. There was a strong campaign against "hyphenation." Identifying oneself as German-American or Irish-American or Italian-American or whatever was seen as a sign of divided loyalties. Such people were regarded as half-Americans. The goal of Americanization became to stamp out hyphenation and create 100 percent Americans. A variety of organizations pursued this goal through the schools, factories, and media. Soon, however, the Ku Klux Klan and other extreme radicals jumped on the Americanization bandwagon, and their hysterical support helped discredit it. Spokesmen from the various immigrant communities began to express their anger at having the Americanizers attempt to destroy the cultural identity of millions of Americans. By the middle of the 1920s, Americanization had been so discredited that it was no longer a major force in society.

ANGLO-SAXON RACIALISM

In the early 1900s, there was another attack on ethnic consciousness which was blatantly racist but tried to mask itself as science. This was Anglo-Saxon racialism. "Anglo-Saxonism was thus closely identified from the first with love of freedom, dedication to republicanism [democracy], and a commitment to law and limited government. Allied to these political qualities were such domestic and personal virtues as respect for womanhood, honesty, simplicity, and bravery."[14]

This summary had long been associated with the central aspects of Anglo-Saxon cultural heritage. Those dedicated to Anglo-Saxon racialism, however, maintained that these qualities were innate to Anglo-Saxons alone. There were those who claimed that scientific studies proved that these qualities were, in fact, a unique part of the genetic makeup of Anglo-Saxons. This, they concluded, meant that Anglo-Saxons were, by nature, the ideal Americans.

Other ethnic groups were "scientifically proven" to be inferior to Anglo-Saxons. In 1910, the Dillingham Commission, appointed by President Theodore Roosevelt, released its forty volume study which purported to prove that southern European immigrants were innately inferior to northern European immigrants. This massive study was reviewed in 1922 by Dr. Harry Laughlin, who concluded that, "Making all logical allowances for environmental conditions, which may be unfavorable . . . the recent immigrants as a whole present a higher percentage of inborn socially inadequate qualities than do the older stocks."[15] Other scientific experts of the day "wrote about the 'remarkable tendency to suicide' among the Japanese in California, 'the strong tendency to delusional trends of persecutory nature' in West Indian Negroes, the frequency of 'hidden sexual complexes' among the Hebrews, and 'the remarkable prevalence of mutism' among Poles."[16] In 1923, Carl Brigham, in his book *A Study of American Intelligence*, asserted that "The representatives of the Alpine and Mediterranean races in our immigration are intellectually inferior to the representatives of the Nordic race."[17] In 1926, Clifford Kirkpatrick concluded that "Definite limits are set by heredity, and immigrants of low innate ability cannot by any amount of Americanization be made into intelligent American citizens capable of appropriating and advancing a complex culture."[18] Southern Europeans, thus, could learn to imitate Anglo-Saxons and thus become Americanized to some extent, though their "innate" deficiencies would keep them from ever totally achieving the ideal. It was further believed by the "experts" that Blacks, Asians, and any other dark-skinned people were utterly unable to imitate Anglo-Saxons and thus were unfit for citizenship.

A variety of organizations such as the Immigration Restriction League were formed to promote the idea "that any heritage other than the 'biologically superior' Anglo-Saxon line of the Founding Fathers would infect and weaken the greatness of America."[19] These organizations were much more than radical fringe groups. Such leading figures of the day as Massachusetts Senator Henry Cabot Lodge, Stanford University president David Starr Jordan, and M.I.T.'s president Francis A. Walker were members of the Immigration Restriction League.[20] While the most strident forms of Anglo-Saxon racialism faded away with the approach of World War II because they sounded so much like the rhetoric of the Nazis, this so-called "science" still had a significant effect on American thinking. The racially restrictive immigration laws of the 1920s, which were adopted to frustrate Asian and southern European immigration, were based on Anglo-Saxon racialist thinking. Indeed it was not until the Immigration Act of 1965 that the last vestige of Anglo-Saxon racialism was finally removed from United States immigration policies.

CULTURAL PLURALISM

Even as Americanization and Anglo-Saxon racialism were dominating the scene there was another concept of ethnic consciousness and identity which was being expressed. This concept, which came to be known as cultural pluralism, was first presented by Horace M. Kallen in the February 1915 issue of *The Nation*. Kallen was firmly anti-assimilationist. He felt it was neither desirable nor possible for all the ethnic communities of the United States to melt into one generic community. He believed that harmony rather than unity should be the goal of a country made up of so many ethnic groups. He saw the United States as an orchestra in which each instrument—that is, each ethnic group—retained its unique sound, and yet, together, all the instruments—all the ethnic groups—produced beautiful music. He envisioned a country where all ethnic groups were encouraged to maintain their ethnic distinctives, including their language if they so desired. All groups, however, would cooperate through certain national political and economic institutions, and the common language of the nation would be English. He encouraged the United States to become a "society whose institutions encourage individuality in groups, in persons, in temperaments, whose program liberates these individualities and guides them into a fellowship of freedom and cooperation."[21] Kallen presented few specifics on how how this cultural harmony could be accomplished, but he did at least put forward the possibility that the United States could function as one nation even while it encouraged ethnic diversity.

Cultural pluralism didn't make much of an impact on the majority of Americans. The melting pot image was by far the dominant image of the day. A small group of intellectuals, however, became convinced that cultural pluralism offered the best way of dealing with the realities of the ethnic diversity of the United States. They kept the idea alive and began conducting studies on ethnic diversity and publishing articles and books which took issue with the melting pot image. Time was on their side.

With the rise of Nazism in Germany and the decline in the United States of the Americanization movement and Anglo-Saxon racialism, the cultural pluralism of Kallen began to gain followers. As time went by, the term "cultural pluralism" began to have meanings Kallen never intended, but in all its expressions it was always a call for celebrating ethnic diversity rather than suppressing it. The ethnic debates of the first quarter of the twentieth century had one lasting impact: they framed the ethnic question in terms of race, nationality, language and cultural distinctives, terms which still define the ethnic debate today.

From the mid 1920s, ethnic concerns began to fade as a national issue. The worst possibilities of Americanization and Anglo-Saxon racialism had been avoided and the various immigrant communities were adapting to the general American culture in ways which gave no cause for alarm. The great crash of 1929 and the prolonged Depression of the 1930s turned people's attention away from ethnic concerns and toward basic economic concerns. Immigration slowed dramatically during this period, so there were no major new ethnic groups to draw attention to ethnicity.

INTERCULTURAL EDUCATION

The rise of Nazism brought ethnic concerns back to center stage. In public education a program was developed called "intercultural education." "There were two themes in intercultural education: the first was that one should not be ashamed of one's heritage; the second and more important was that all should be tolerant of racial, religious, and cultural differences."[22] Intercultural education was an American response to the Aryan superiority and racial hatred themes of Nazism.

NAZISM, WORLD WAR II AND ETHNICITY IN AMERICA

Nazism, with its strident themes of racial hatred, reminded America that one of its great virtues was its diversity. In opposition to the Nazi "master race" doctrine, the nation reaffirmed that the foundation of American identity was an ideological commitment, not membership in a particular racial or ethnic group. Every ethnic group in the

United States had reason to oppose Nazism and support the war effort. Because of this, World War II did not cause suspicion to be directed toward the various immigrant communities. The major exception to this was, of course, the Japanese-American community, which suffered greatly because of its ethnicity. World War II proved that the United States, in spite of its ethnic diversity, had an underlying unity which could sustain it through a long and costly war effort. Over 12 million young men and women from every ethnic background served in the armed forces during the War. Not only did this prove the loyalty of the many ethnic groups, but the war experience itself was the first close contact many in this country had with people from other ethnic backgrounds. From the shared experiences of the War came a deep conviction that, in spite of their differences, all Americans shared basic values. When the soldiers came home at the end of the war, many had been permanently changed in their understanding of other ethnic groups.

WORLD WAR II AND ITS EFFECT ON
AFRICAN-AMERICAN ETHNIC CONSCIOUSNESS

In the aftermath of the War, the true horror of the master race philosophy of the Nazis became evident. The entire country recoiled at the evil revealed. This brought about a reaffirmation among the American people that all races, nationalities, and religions were welcome to share the blessings of liberty. Most, of course, thought only of white ethnic groups when they affirmed this. African-Americans, however, were listening. The War had brought them, as well as the rest of the United States, to a new understanding of this country's ethnically inclusive nature.

In 1944, the Swedish social scientist Gunnar Myrdal's book, titled *An American Dilemma*, was published. This book was an intensive study on the African-American community, its situation at the time, and its prospects for the future.

Myrdal foresaw that the War would permanently alter the consciousness of African America and the way it would relate to the rest of the country in the future. Here's how he assessed the situation:

> America can never more regard its Negroes as a patient, submissive minority. They will continually become less well 'accommodated.' They will organize for defense and offense. They will be more and more vociferous . . . . They will have a powerful tool in the caste struggle against white America: the glorious American ideals of democracy, liberty, and equality to which America is pledged not only by its political Constitution but also by the sincere devotion of its citizens. The Negroes are a minority, and they are poor and suppressed, but they have the advantage that they can fight wholeheartedly. The whites have all the power, but they are split in their moral personality. Their better selves are with the insurgents. The Negroes do not need any other allies.[23]

Myrdal's insights, which he framed before the War actually began, would prove prophetic.

ETHNICITY IN THE 1940s AND 1950s

The immediate aftermath of the War brought no major changes to the United States. From the mid 1940s to the mid 1950s, ethnic consciousness seemed at a low ebb again. The economy was experiencing its post-war boom, and that occupied everyone's mind. The McCarran-Walter Immigration and Nationality Act of 1952 relaxed some of the racial and national origins restrictions of earlier legislation, but it had no dramatic effect on the ethnic makeup of the country. It was also a time when various politicians connected with the House Un-American Actitivies Committee were looking for Communists everywhere. Anyone who didn't seem to be mainstream American could easily be branded a Communist. It was not a safe time to express diversity of any kind.

THE AFRICAN-AMERICAN CIVIL RIGHTS MOVEMENT AND ETHNIC CONSCIOUSNESS

In the late 1950s, Myrdal's predictions began to be realized as the Civil Rights Movement gained national stature. First, African-Americans demanded as their Constitutional right equal access to the country's educational institutions. There followed the crusade to wipe away all the entrenched legal and social barriers preventing them from enjoying all the blessings of freedom. The 1964 Civil Rights Act was the legislative capstone of this crusade. This legislation not only ensured their birthright as Americans, but assured the same for all other ethnic groups.

Even as this crusade was moving forward, another, born in the mid 1960s, was beginning. This crusade emphasized Black ethnic consciousness, Black pride, Black power, and finally, for the extremists in the movement, Black separatism. As African-Americans demanded and received their rights and celebrated their ethnicity, other groups began movements to assert themselves and their claims. Hispanics, Native Americans, and Asians (to a lesser degree) began to ask the United States to let all its people participate equally in its life and its freedoms. Ethnic distinctives long suppressed were openly expressed. These ethnic struggles were sometimes marked by misunderstandings, over-statements and, at times, violence. The result, however, was a country that was making the ethnic inclusiveness embodied in its Constitution and in the poem on the base of the Statue of Liberty a reality for more and more of its people.

Though many Anglos objected to the Civil Rights Movement and its results in other non-white ethnic communities, those movements had at least one positive impact. Many Anglos became concerned with their own ethnic roots. This led to a general reawakening of interest in ethnicity throughout the United States. Many Anglos watched the epochal television miniseries "Roots" with as much fascination as did the African-Americans.

The 1970s, however, showed that there was also a negative side to this new ethnicity. As each group asserted its uniqueness and developed its own agenda, there was less certainty about what the country as a whole stood for. This showed itself in several ways. There was a weakening of commitment to national social issues as each group became concerned only with its own issues. Election patterns in the 1970s indicated that the United States wasn't sure what it wanted from its leaders. With few positive national issues to address, politics tended to degenerate into pettiness. Special interests were beginning to harm the national interest. Foreign policy also seemed mired in uncertainty. Our leaders seemed unable to decide whether to pursue aggressively our vision of what the world should be, or to turn away from international issues and concentrate on domestic issues.

THE 1980s TO THE PRESENT: INCREASING DIVERSITY AND CONCERNS ABOUT DIVERSITY

In 1980, with the election of President Reagan, the country signaled that it was ready to go back to simpler times when the upheavals and complexities of the 1960s and 1970s had not yet occurred. In the 1980s, ethnicity was again controversial. In our national motto, *E pluribus unum*, many wanted to concentrate on the *unum*. But it was not possible to turn back the clock. Diversity was a fact of life. There was much debate about whether this diversity was good or bad for the country, but no amount of wishing would make it go away.

The Immigration Act of 1965 abolished the national origins quota system and the bias against Asia and Africa. This truly opened the United States to the world, and perhaps most important, it signaled the beginning of large scale Asian and African immigration. Once again, as in the late 1800s and early 1900s, new immigrants—immigrants who were very different from their counterparts in the past—streamed into the nation. Most of them settled in large, highly visible, urban enclaves, especially on the east and west coasts. Continuing social and political upheavals throughout the world brought more and more people to the United States as refugees. Most of these refugees were from the so-called "Third World." Many of these immigrants and refugees were non-white and seemed unwilling or unable to assimilate quickly into mainstream society. While many longed for a return to the more homogeneous 1940s and 1950s, the heightened sensitivity to ethnic concerns brought about by the 1960s and 1970s prevented any serious attempt at forced assimilation. Though some stridently xenophobic voices were raised and the Ku Klux Klan experienced an increase in membership, there was no repeat of the excesses of the Americanization movement or Anglo-Saxon racialism. The rights of these new groups to maintain their ethnic identity were generally affirmed.

As we move into the 1990s, the debate over ethnic identity is still quite lively. Some fear that the recently arrived ethnic groups will degrade our national life, take jobs away from the native-born, and ultimately destroy our traditional identity as a nation upheld by northern European cultural and social structures. These are the same concerns expressed in the late 1800s and early 1900s about the Chinese and the southern and eastern Europeans. Others welcome the newcomers and expect that they, like all the other groups before them, will enrich rather than destroy our national character. As we move toward the twenty-first century, we can expect this debate, which is over 200 years old, to continue to heat up to the point where it could become quite divisive.

A WORD TO THE CHURCH

Throughout our history, we Americans have wrestled with two poles of tension: our oneness as a nation and our diversity as a people. With so many new refugees and immigrants this tension will continue to escalate. We in the church need to establish a ministry philosophy which will be sensitive to the issues raised by this debate and have something constructive and biblically responsible to add to it. Also, as Christians, we are part of a movement that stresses both unity and diversity within the Body of Christ. A clear understanding of unity and diversity as they apply both to our nation and to our church is necessary if we are to minister sensitively to the new Americans as they seek to come to terms with our national culture without surrendering their ethnic uniqueness.

DISCUSSION QUESTIONS

1. Are you basically pluralist or nonpluralist, and why?

2. Throughout our history, what have been the recurrent fears of many regarding each new wave of immigrants and/or refugees? Do you think these fears influence your spiritual concern for the recently arrived immigrants and refugees? If so, how?

3. Describe and contrast the "melting pot" and "cultural pluralism" concepts. How do you react to each of them?

4. How did the African-American civil rights movement affect all other ethnic groups in this country? How were you influenced by this movement?

5.   Do you think the Christian church has been influenced by the Americanization Movement and Anglo-Saxon racialism? Explain. Have you been influenced by them? If so, how?

4

ETHNICITY, AMERICAN IDENTITY, AND THE ROLE OF ETHNICITY IN THE CHRISTIAN CHURCH

After some 200 years of debating the subject of ethnicity and American identity, a three-layered understanding has emerged. American identity is composed of an ideological commitment to the concepts of liberty, equality, and democracy, unique ethnic identity, and the shared history in America of the group or individual.

THE THREE LAYERS OF THE AMERICAN IDENTITY

The first layer of the American identity is common to all, regardless of ethnic background or time spent in this country. To be an American means to support the ideals of liberty, equality, and democracy as described in our Constitution and expressed through our governmental structures and social patterns. These values inspired the American Revolution. Throughout our history, millions of Americans have fought, sacrificed, and died defending them. Our political debates may become heated, but they are always conducted within the framework of these values. Our society may change dramatically, as it did because of the Civil Rights Movement, but the changes are always given shape by these values. Our nation may struggle to find answers to difficult questions, such as rising crime rates, but the possible answers are limited to those which are compatible with these values. Since the values of liberty, equality, and democracy are so central to our identity as Americans, it is impossible to think of a person wanting citizenship in the United States or functioning as a responsible citizen without a commitment to them. Therefore, whatever a person's ethnic background and whatever the guiding principles of his homeland

108

might be, if he wants to become an American, he must have a commitment to the basic values of this nation. These are the values which create unity in a nation as diverse in as ours. Indeed, they make it possible for him or her to become an American without surrendering his or her ethnicity. At first, this commitment may be primarily theoretical, with little understanding of how basic these values are to the whole culture. Gradually, the commitment is deepened by practical experience and greater awareness of their implications. To be sure, various ethnic groups will have their unique ways of understanding these values, but once they are committed to them, their input becomes a part of the continuing debate on how best to live up to our ideals.

The second layer of the American identity is ethnicity. The various groups which have come to America have brought with them their unique ethnic identities. Some came with only a local or regional identity and discovered in the United States their larger ethnic identity. They did not have to shed this identity in order to become Americans, since American identity is basically ideological and not ethnic. The only limiting factor was that no ethnic expression was permitted to do violence to the the basic American values of liberty, equality, and democracy.

Though there were times in our history when ethnic identity became suspect and there have been groups which have advocated the eradication of ethnic identity, ethnicity has always been and always will be a part of the United States. Ethnic identity, far from being a liability, is a resource by which ethnics find responsible ways of fitting into the American mosaic. Indeed, certain recent studies have suggested that ethnicity may well be beneficial for the whole society. These studies show that a slow rate of assimilation by newly arrived ethnics into the larger American culture is preferable to a rapid rate.

Rapid assimilation can extract a heavy emotional toll. Those who rapidly assimilate have more problems with "alcohol and drug abuse or dependence, phobia, and antisocial personality"[1] than those who assimilate slowly. If a newly arrived ethnic attempts to assimilate very rapidly, he tends to become lost between two cultures. He cuts himself off from his native culture and thus loses the stabilizing influences of its social structures, behavior patterns, and basic understanding of life. He embraces certain aspects of American culture, but does so in a rather haphazard way. What he embraces does not add up to an integrated system which can give him the skills he needs to cope with the complexities and difficulties of life. Without adequate cultural resources, he is likely to have a variety of emotional and personality difficulties. The ethnic who assimilates slowly continues to be nourished by his native culture as he comes to terms with his new culture. This nourishment gives him the stability he needs to avoid much of the emotional trauma of adapting to life in a new culture. As time goes by, he finds that rather than being lost between two cultures he is being nourished by two cultures.

It is also as members of ethnically conscious groups that new immigrants and refugees learn about how things are done in the United States. Ethnic groups in this country soon develop a political and social agenda. This agenda is at first quite narrow and focused on their unique concerns. As they utilize the American political system, "by mobilizing the collective vote and by electing their own to office, immigrant minorities have learned the rules of the democratic game and absorbed its values in the process."[2] As they participate in the democratic process, they soon discover the necessity of working with other groups on issues of common concern and slowly develop an outlook which goes beyond their own ethnic group and pulls them toward the mainstream.

Ethnic identity is, then, something much more than a nuisance which must be shed as quickly as possible. It provides an important resource for people as they become contributing members of American society. This was true for the Germans, Irish, Italians, and others who came in generations past, and it's just as true of the Hispanics, Asians, Africans, and others who have come recently.

The third layer of the American identity is the shared history in the United States, which affects the life of each new immigrant and refugee from the day he arrives in this country. The sights, sounds, social customs, legal system, governmental structures, recreational life, food, political debates, and the reaction of others to his presence, combined with many other factors, gradually pull him into a culture different from his own and common to millions of his fellow Americans. As time goes by, each individual and each ethnic group gradually shares deeper and deeper in the life and history of all Americans.

The relationship between a person's ethnic identity and his shared American history experience is quite dynamic. It could be described in two different ways. First, when a person initially arrives, he begins at zero in the shared American history category, but from the very beginning he is influenced by life in his new country. As time goes by, he shares more experiences with all his fellow Americans, and those experiences influence his basic identity. He still retains his ethnic identity, but he also gradually acquires identity based on his experiences here. The more time he spends in the United States, the more of his identity will be shaped by his shared American history experience and the less will be shaped by his ethnic identity. The same can be said for entire ethnic groups. The illustration below shows how this process works.

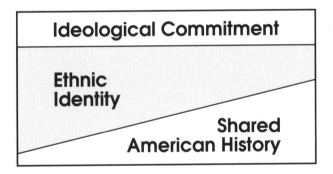

The process, however, is not as simple or as predictable as this illustration suggests. There are five complicating variables. First is the distance and degree of isolation from the culture of origin or homeland. When the homeland is near, there is generally continued contact with its people, culture and language. This continued contact will lessen the influence of the shared history in America and will give continued importance to ethnic identity. When the homeland is far away, the group may have little continuing contact with it. Even if the distance is not that great, political circumstances may prevent significant continuing contact. Where contact is minimal there is generally a steady lessening of ethnic identity and a steady increase in identity with the larger American culture. Also, when there is little contact with the homeland, what culture is preserved will be the culture as it was when the group left for the United States. The cultural development of the homeland will not be reflected in the American ethnic community.

Again, things are not as simple as they first appear. Refugees may be thousands of miles from their homeland and have little chance of ever returning, but they may still dream of returning, and this dream has great power. It will increase their tendency to separate themselves as much as possible from mainstream culture, and this lessens the impact of their shared history in the United States. Since they dream of returning to their homeland, they concentrate on preserving their culture of origin—for they see it, and not American culture, as the culture of their future.

A unique factor of today's immigrants and refugees is the speed, ease, and economy of world-wide travel. In the great immigrations of the 1800s, the immigrants, once here, almost never had an opportunity to return to their homeland. Today's immigrants can quickly and comfortably return for repeated visits to their distant homelands, and many do. This continuing contact tends to reinforce the culture of origin, even if that culture is thousands of miles away, and lessen the influence of shared history in America.

Secondly, the kind of reception a group receives in this country also influences the rate at which shared history in the United States influences it and pulls it toward the mainstream. A group which encounters hospitality upon its arrival will tend to be open to the assimilating effects of its shared history experiences. A group which encounters hostility will tend to withdraw into tightly knit ethnic enclaves and insulate itself from the assimilating effects of shared American history. Indeed, hostile encounters as a major component of shared American history may well harden a group's resolve not to assimilate in any way. Many non-white groups have received and continue to receive a very hostile reception in this country. This helps to explain why many of them have maintained a high degree of ethnicity. Racial prejudice has hindered the development of a significant shared American history dimension in their identity.

A third variable is the social and economic class mix of a group. Groups which are made up mainly of manual laborers tend to be less influenced by shared history in America than those made up mainly of members of the entrepreneurial and professional classes. The manual labor class may have had little knowledge of American culture before arriving here and their limited job skills tend to concentrate them in certain sectors of the economy where they relate primarily with others from their ethnic group. Entrepreneurial ethnics, like the manual laborers, may have had little contact with American culture before their arrival and usually begin by providing goods and services to and employment for primarily their own group. However, many soon develop business contacts beyond their group and begin serving clientele from a variety of ethnic backgrounds. Because of these experiences, their perspectives are broadened. Their shared history in the United States pulls them toward the mainstream. Members of the professional class have often had significant contact with American culture prior to their arrival through their education and professional associations. When they arrive, they soon identify more strongly with others in their profession than others in their ethnic group. Also, their professions tend to disperse them throughout the society. This professional identity and spatial dispersion tends to make their shared history a powerful force in their lives from the begining of their American experience. Thus, the mix of these three types of people in a group influences how quickly and profoundly the group as a whole is influenced by their shared history in America.

The fourth variable relates to the size of the ethnic group. Large groups tend to create their own communities in their adopted country which recreate the life and culture of their country of origin. Such large ethnic enclaves lessen the impact of shared history in the United States— almost as though they exist alongside the mainstream culture but have no real connection to it. Small ethnic groups do not have the numbers necessary to recreate the life and culture of their country of origin. As a result, they are forced to relate to the larger culture almost from the beginning and are deeply affected by it.

The fifth variable is the degree of cultural difference between an ethnic group and mainstream American culture. Groups with a European cultural heritage find in the United States a culture similar to their own. It is relatively easy for them to incorporate aspects of their new culture into their identities without significantly challenging their culture of origin. Because of this cultural similarity, the shared American history dimension of their identity grows quickly and they move quickly into the mainstream of American life. Groups from non-European backgrounds find in North America a culture profoundly different from their own. It is difficult for them to incorporate significant aspects of their new culture into their identities without rejecting signficant aspects of their culture of origin. Because of this cultural clash the shared American history dimension of their identities grows slowly and they move slowly into the cultural mainstream.

Because of these factors, the illustration on page 107, though useful, is simplistic. No single graph can accurately describe the interplay of ethnic identity and shared American history in every ethnic group. Each group would have to be graphed separately, taking into consideration its relationship with its country of origin, its positive and negative experiences in the United States, its socio-economic class mix, its size, and its degree of cultural difference from mainstream American culture.

There is a second way of looking at the interrelationship of ethnic identity and shared American history. This is to look at the way these two are related during the first three generations in the United States. In 1938, Marcus L. Hansen, in his book *The Problem of the Third Generation Immigrant*, explored the different ways in which the immigrant, his son and grandson dealt with their ethnic identity and mainstream American culture. Hansen summed up his perception of the differences between the three generations in the phrase, "What the son wishes to forget, the grandson wishes to remember."[3] Margaret Mead, among others, picked up on Hansen's ideas. In 1955, Will Herberg built on Hansen's insights in his book *Protestant—Catholic—Jew.*[4] Herberg's book dealt with the seemingly contradictary trends of the 1950s, when both church membership and the secularization of society were on the increase. Herberg's thesis was that the surge in church membership was more the result of the grandchildren of the immigrant generation searching for their ethnic roots than a revival of spirituality. What follows is a brief summary of the three–generation unfolding and reshaping of ethnic awareness first proposed by Hansen.

The immigrant generation generally acquires a low degree of shared American history and retains a high degree of ethnic identity. This is due partly to the tendency of first generation immigrants to gather in ethnic communities, partly to the language barrier which tends to separate them from those who speak English, and partly to their lack of interest in participating in general American life and culture. The ethnicity of the first generation tends to keep it a stranger in its new land. Rarely, if ever, do first generation ethnics function comfortably in mainstream American culture.

The second generation tends to embrace American culture and seeks to become deeply involved in the shared American history experience. They don't want to learn the language of the old country and don't want to continue customs which would set them apart. They generally seek to become Americanized, and this usually causes strains in families and in the entire immigrant community.

The third generation tends to have a renewed interest in their ethnic identity. There is a return to ethnic consciousness, but as Nathan Glazar reminds us, this return "is to something quite different from what was there before."[5] They don't want to retreat into ethnic communities and separate themselves by language from the rest of America, but they do want to learn about their ethnic heritage and to find meaningful ways to express that heritage. This is not an attempt to disconnect from the larger culture, nor is it an expression of renewed loyalty to the ancestral homeland. It is simply an enrichment of their identity as Americans; a way of establishing their place in the American mosaic.

This kind of interest in ethnic identity usually becomes a permanent part of the group's larger American identity. In groups that maintain a high degree of group cohesion, such as Chinese and Koreans, the community as a whole decides how it wants to express its ethnic identity. Most of its members will then share a common understanding of the importance of maintaining the agreed upon amount of ethnic identity. In groups which have little group cohesion, such as German-Americans, the decisions on ethnicity are usually made on the family or individual level. Based on those decisions the family or individual seeks out and participates in ethnic activities which are of interest. The illustration below shows the relationship, by generation, of ethnic identity to shared

American history. Again it must be noted that this illustration, like the preceeding one, is useful but simplistic. The same variables highlighted in relationship to the illustration above apply to the illustration below.

Interest in Ethnic Identity	Interest in Ethnic Identity	Interest in Ethnic Identity
	Interest in Shared American History	Interest in Shared American History
Interest in Shared American History		
1st Generation	2nd Generation	3rd Generation

These two ways of looking at the relationship between ethnic identity and shared American history are not mutually exclusive. The first shows the general pattern of an ethnic group's identity being shaped and changed by its shared history. It is generally true that the longer a group has been this country, the more profoundly its identity is influenced by general American culture. The second way explains why the ethnic identity part of the total identity shrinks but doesn't disappear. Because of our nation's toleration and even celebration of diversity, most groups maintain some type of ethnic awareness. The pattern of ethnic awareness may not conform to the three–generation pattern of the second graph. The ethnic awareness, unconcern, and reawakening may be played out over a period of more than three generations. In certain instances, there may be no generation which is unconcerned about ethnicity. The second illustration attempts to explain the persistence of ethnic consciousness shown in the first illustration.

Another fact worth noting is that each major group of new Americans alters, to some degree, the American identity. As American culture changes them profoundly, they change it subtly. This is a process which has been at work for more than 200 years. Because of this ongoing process, ours is a very fluid culture. No definition of what it means to be an American is ever final. We are constantly re-inventing ourselves based on the changing makeup of our ethnic mosaic. This is what makes American culture, a culture shaped by so many ethnic groups, so dynamic and lively. Those who fear the changes our newest ethnic groups might cause need to remember that their ancestors altered American culture without destroying it. The new groups will do the same thing. They will change American culture, not by destroying something already here, but by adding to and enriching what they find. Holding on to past definitions of what it means to be an American will leave us ill–prepared to deal with the United States in the 1990s and beyond.

THE ROLE OF ETHNICITY IN THE AMERICAN IDENTITY

There are a variety of ideas about the most desirable role of ethnicity in the American identity. They form a continuum which ranges from no toleration of ethnicity to ethnicity as a factor which rightly separates each group from the others. I will touch on seven ideas. In certain contexts, some of these terms have meanings different from those I will be giving.

Americanization as used here refers to the ideas advanced by those in the Americanization Movement which flourished during the first quarter of the twentieth century. While that movement has been discredited as a workable way of dealing with ethnic identity, Americanization ideas are still floating around in some quarters today. Americanization asks ethnics to shed completely their ethnicity in order to become Americans. It suspects that anyone who expresses ethnic identity is less than loyal to the United States. It resents any aspect of American society which is not rooted in Anglo-Saxon culture and opposes the incorporation of any cultural aspects of the new ethnic groups. It is especially zealous in demanding that ethnics not only learn to speak English but also discontinue any public use of their former language. Americanization is impatient with ethnic groups and wants them to shed their ethnicity even during the first generation.

One note of explanation. The terms "Americanize" and "Americanization" can be used in a neutral way to describe the process of ethnics adapting to American culture. Thus we say a Vietnamese-American is becoming Americanized when he wears jeans. We do not mean by this that he has shed his ethnicity, but that he is adopting American ways. In such a context, those terms lack any ideological content. They are merely descriptive.

Assimilation is similar to Americanization but is not nearly as aggressive. Assimilation proceeds more from a utilitarian point of view than an ideological point of view. Americanization sees ethnicity as disloyal to a particular brand of American patriotism. Assimilation sees ethnicity as counterproductive to the harmony of society. Assimilation believes the harmony of society is threatened when people cherish their ethnicity. Society, conversely, becomes more harmonious as less ethnicity is expressed. Therefore the best society is one in which ethnicity is not expressed and where everyone adopts the values of Anglo-American culture. Admittedly, this view of the preferred society as one in which Anglo-American culture triumphs over all is ideologically based. Its foundation rests in the age-old dream of creating a "new man" in the "new world." It does not, however, have the "true believer" intolerance of Americanization ideology. Assimilation is more patient than Americanization. It believes that if Anglo-American culture exerts constant pressure on ethnics, they will gradually lose their ethnicity and function harmoniously with the rest of society. Thus the goals of Americanization and assimilation are similar. The difference is that Americanization demands that ethnics reject their ethnicity before they can be considered American, while assimilation asks ethnics to let go of their ethnicity for the good of society.

Again, as with "Americanization," the term "assimilation" can be simply a descriptive term. It can be used to describe how an ethnic group comes to terms with the larger American culture, with no agenda for how that process must unfold.

Acculturation asks for less than a complete abandonment of ethnicity but is still opposed to any group's desire to maintain a significant public ethnic identity. Acculturation asks ethnics to fit into Anglo-American culture and to sacrifice any part of their ethnicity which would set them apart, in any significant way, from others. Since these ideals are subjective, there is considerable debate as to how much ethnicity is welcome. Generally speaking, acculturation is only tolerant of a very low level of ethnic identity. It asks that most ethnic expressions be confined to the ethnic community or the family so as not to have an effect on the larger society. It would accept certain aspects of an ethnic culture being visible in the general culture, such as ethnic food and perhaps certain celebrations. It would oppose any ethnic expression which could be viewed as an expression of commitment to the ethnic community's place of origin. Many view acculturation as a way-station on the journey to complete assimilation. Most Anglos would prefer assimilation as the way in which ethnics deal with their ethnicity. Most ethnics, especially first generation ethnics, prefer acculturation. They will accomodate the larger society by restraining certain ethnic expressions, thus satisfying the concerns of acculturation, but will accomodate only as much as is necessary to keep from being held in suspicion.

Toleration asks that ethnicity be permitted as a fact of life. Each group has its distinctives and those distinctives should be respected so long as they do not appear to cause serious conflicts in society. There is no sense of celebrating ethnicity, but there is a commitment to permit each group to express ethnicity. To attempt to destroy ethnicity would harm society more than to tolerate it. While it would set definite limits to ethnic expressions, toleration would allow considerable freedom within those limits.

Cultural integration has a positive feeling about ethnicity. Ethnicity is to be celebrated as an important part of America's greatness. While it allows wide latitude for ethnic expression, it also asks ethnics to take seriously their commitment to the American ideals of liberty, equality and democracy and to value the part of their history they now share with all other Americans. Cultural integration does not seek to take something away from an ethnic group to make them acceptable, but to add something to what they already possess. Without destroying their ethnic identity which gives them uniqueness, cultural integration seeks to add a loyalty to the basic American ideals so that they will feel a unity with all other Americans.

Cultural pluralism is very close to cultural integration. Both concepts owe much to the ideas of Horace Kallen. While cultural integration would see the ideological commitment to liberty, equality, and democracy as the center of one's identity, cultural pluralism generally sees ethnic identity as the center. Cultural pluralism doesn't ignore the ideological layer of the American identity, but it doesn't stress it to any great degree. It places great value on ethnic identity and asks the larger society to celebrate every kind of ethnic expression. It allows each ethnic group to decide how strong an ethnic identity it wants to maintain and then defends that level of ethnicity even if it causes disruption in society.

Cultural separatism seeks to insulate ethnic groups from being changed by general American culture. It believes that each ethnic group should be encouraged to maintain a strong ethnic identity, including its language. Furthermore, it would separate groups geographically so they could express their ethnicity without compromise. It would ask the United States to make whatever changes are necessary in order to make this a nation of semi-autonomous states. Cultural separatism has never been an idea which commanded much loyalty in the United States. It has had significant impact in Canada and led to a French-speaking Quebec. It is also at work in the disintegration/re-formation of the Soviet Union and several other Eastern European countries.

CULTURAL INTEGRATION APPLIED TO THE UNITY—DIVERSITY DEBATE

These, then, are the options before us as a nation as we decide how we will deal with the many ethnic groups within our borders. Our unity as a nation is important. If we are to function as a major player in world events, we must have a strong center. If we are to have domestic peace, all the groups that make up this nation must be joined by some sense of unity. At the same time, a central factor in the genius of our country is our diversity. This diversity cannot be ignored or suppressed without harming who we are as a people. The church faces a similar situation. As we move into ministry with various ethnic groups, we must decide how we will adapt to ethnic diversity and how we will maintain our historic identity. The decisions we make will affect how we relate to ethnics, what kind of churches we encourage various ethnic groups to develop, and even what kind of a future we have.

CULTURAL INTEGRATION AND ETHNICITY
IN AMERICAN SOCIETY

In the national arena, it is my belief that the idea which holds the most promise for affirming our oneness as a nation and our ethnic diversity is cultural integration. Cultural integration recognizes that there must be a unifying factor in our identity as Americans which will allow us to function as one people. We have rightly rejected race, national origin, or religion as our unifying principle and have chosen loyalty to the Constitutional ideals of liberty, equality, and democracy. Cultural integration takes this unifying ideological commitment seriously. Regardless of your ethnic identity, to be an American and to function positively in American society, you must have a commitment to the basic ideology upon which this country is built. Some have tended to elevate this basic ideology to the level of a civil religion which supplants all other religions. While this is a danger we need to guard against, we still recognize the value of having a strong ideological foundation upon which to construct our national unity.

Having affirmed a strong unifying factor for all Americans, cultural integration affirms the right of all people to cherish, express, and celebrate their ethnicity in whatever ways *they* choose. We do not require a person to have a high degree of ethnic consciousness, but neither do we discourage it. Cultural integration asks our nation to celebrate its diversity, not be embarrassed by it. Remember our national motto: *E pluribus unum.* Since it has a strong sense of *unum*, our nation is free to have a strong sense of *pluribus* also.

Perhaps the best illustration of cultural integration is that of the human body. It is one body with many parts, ruled over by the head. The head corresponds to the ideological commitment to liberty, equality, and democracy. The various parts correspond to the various ethnic groups, each having its own identity, and yet each, by virtue of its connection with the head, working for the benefit of the entire body.

CULTURAL INTEGRATION AND ETHNICITY IN THE
CHURCH

    I would suggest that the model of cultural integration could
be used fruitfully in the Christian church. One biblical picture of
the church is the Body of Christ. St. Paul says Christ "is the head
of the body, the church."(Col. 1:18) Christ is the unifying factor
of the church. In 1 Corinthians, St. Paul says, "The body is a unit,
though it is made up of many parts . . . . Now the body is not
made up of one part, but of many . . . . If they were all one part,
where would the body be? As it is, there are many parts, but one
body . . . . Now you are are the body of Christ, and each one of
you is a part of it," (1 Cor. 12:12, 14, 19, 20 27). Because Christ
joins all of us in a Spirit-given unity, we are each free to be unique,
Spirit-gifted people. This picture of the church, then, establishes the
principle that in the church we participate in a grand unity while
retaining our individual uniqueness.

    While this picture is generally used to affirm each
individual's uniqueness within the unity of the church, it would
seem to be faithful to Scripture to use this same picture to illustrate
a biblical model for the role of ethnic groups in the church. Christ
is the head of the church and each ethnic group is a unique part of
the Body of Christ. All groups find unity at the cross and the empty
tomb. Christ makes us one. Each group is unique because each
group, under the guidance of the Spirit, brings special insights and
strengths which the whole Body needs if it is to be more than a
one-dimensional picture. Our uniqueness as creations of our
heavenly Father gives us, as individuals and groups, a diversity
which enhances the Body of Christ.

    The illustration below shows how the Body of Christ
concept applies to ethnic diversity in the church. It is quite
self-evident but important. You will notice that the head is Christ,
not the Anglo members of the denomination. Those members are
but one part of the Body. We need to implement this idea fully if
we are to be successful in the multi-ethnic United States. We will
not succeed if we in the church insist on controlling Hispanic or
Asian or Black ministry. We have the economic power and the
numerical dominance to do so, but we do not have the biblical
mandate. If we are to be true to the biblical mandate we must

carefully structure our church so that Christ alone, and no single ethnic group, including our own, is normative for the entire chruch. This kind of a church is not only faithful to the biblical model but is also in tune with the direction our nation is moving today. It is a spiritual outworking of cultural integration and as such is culturally appropriate for the current social context of America.

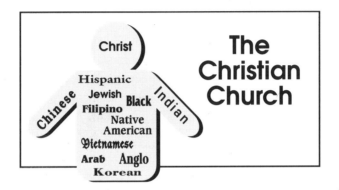

IMPLICATIONS OF
THE CULTURAL INTEGRATION MODEL OF THE
CHURCH
ON THE LOCAL, REGIONAL, AND NATIONAL LEVELS

On the local level, there are five models available as churches seek to live out the cultural integration understanding of the church in ethnically diverse areas.

1. The Multicultural Congregation. In this model, two or more ethnic groups work within the same congregational structure and develop a ministry which meets the needs of all their constituent groups. There are two dangers in this model. First, if the church has a significant Anglo membership, it may simply be a place where ethnics shed their ethnicity and adopt all the trappings of Anglo culture and spirituality. This kind of situation may be appropriate in certain instances, but in most cases assimilationist churches are not attractive to people who value their ethnic identity. Second, if two or more ethnically conscious groups try to cooperate in the same congregational structure, there may be serious strains as each group gives its unique and often contrasting answer to every question faced by the congregation. The congregation may be left without any well-defined identity or sense of mission, since the groups cannot agree in significant areas.

2. The Congregation Within a Congregation. In this model, a monoethnic church responds to the influx into its community of people from a different ethnic group by creating a new church structure which can minister to the unique needs of the new group. It functions within the constitutional organization of the creating church but has its own identity as a specialized ministry. The creating church helps develop the ministry of the new church. There are two dangers with this model also. The first is that the creating church will control the ethnic ministry in ways which meet the expectations of the creating church but fail to meet the needs of the new ethnic group. The second is that the ethnics may pursue their ethnicity in ways which are needlessly threatening to the creating church. Each group, in this situation, will have to work hard so that cross–cultural misunderstandings don't hinder or destroy the relationship.

3. The Partner Congregation. In this model, a monoethnic church facilitates the creation of a new church which can reach people of a specific ethnic group. This new church uses the facilities of the parent church for ministry and may be partially funded by it. From the beginning the new ethnic church is separately constituted and makes all its own decisions. The two churches cooperate as equal partners in certain ways, but in most areas they function independently. In this model, as in the previous one, the two groups must work hard so that cross–cultural misunderstandings do not hinder or destroy the relationship.

4. The "Multi–ethnic, Mutually Autonomous"[6] Congregation. In this model, several autonomous ethnic congregations function under an umbrella organizational structure which administers the finance, ministry, and church polity of all the groups. "Each church has its own congregation, pastor, and lay leaders. Periodically, all the components of the umbrella church worship and engage in common ministries."[7] The umbrella organizational structure is controlled equally or proportionately by representatives of all the churches. In two important aspects, this model comes closest to the cultural integration concept. First, it prevents one group from controlling the ministry of the other. This encourages all groups to look to Christ as Lord of the church. Second, it keeps all the groups relating to each other so that—within a context which respects each group's uniqueness—all the groups can discover their basic Spirit-given unity.

5. *The Church Planting Congregation.* In this model, a monoethnic church assists in the development of a new ethnic church either, nearby or in some other community. There is never any organizational connection between the two churches. The new church begins as a house church or rents facilities in the community. It may or may not have any connection with the facilities of the sponsoring church. If it begins by utilizing the sponsoring church's facilities, that is seen as a temporary arrangement. As soon as finances permit, it purchases or rents its own facility. This model involves minimal contact between the memberships of the two congregations and thus limits the dangers of cross–cultural misunderstandings. It also, however, deprives the two groups of the enriching experiences of significant cross-cultural interchanges. While the two groups may come to appreciate their ethnic diversity, they may never discover their Christian unity.

There is no single right way to minister in a multi-ethnic community. Each of the five models discussed can achieve the cultural integration concept of the church if it is developed carefully and matched with the proper situation.

The critically important question is, "Which model is the best in the present situation?" Each congregation must seriously wrestle with that question before it chooses a model for its outreach. No book can provide the answer for them. Only the guidance of the Spirit can lead to the right answer.

On the regional and national levels, the cultural integration model of the church can be expressed in three ways. First, there should be organizations which link all the congregations of each ethnic group. These organizations fulfill two roles. They facilitate the sharing of ideas and resources among the congregations of the group. They also allow it to address ministry issues on the regional and denominational levels. These organizations should be encouraged by denominational leaders, and their input on ministry issues should be carefully considered.

Second, people from various ethnic groups should be represented at all levels and in all areas of the governmental structure of the denomination. This is not a call for quotas. It is a call to recognize the leadership potential of people from all ethnic groups and to help develop that leadership potential through culture–specific programs.

Third, there should be a statistically significant number of pastors and teachers from the various ethnic groups which make up a denomination. They can function as leaders of their religious communities and assist in their development. We should vigorously recruit prospective candidates for the preaching and teaching ministry from a variety of ethnic groups. In some cases, the recruitment programs currently used in Anglo situations may have to be changed significantly to be effective with other groups. Preparatory schools need to create programs which will assure ethnic students the resources they need to acclimate to an environment which may feel alien to them. We also need to provide specialized programs which can prepare ethnic students for the academic regimen of denominational schools.

Developing a denomination which expresses the cultural integration model of the church as illustrated above will take time and effort. We have a long way to go. We have so deeply connected our theology and our northern European cultural traditions that we have been resistant to those who have asked us to be open to expressions of Christianity which proceed from non-European cultural traditions. Since attempts to open the church to mainstream Anglo-American culture have often been controversial,[8] it is obvious that opening the church to the influence of African, Asian, and Hispanic culture will be quite difficult.

CREATING APPROPRIATE EXPRESSIONS OF CHRISTIANITY IN NEW CULTURES

The cultural integration model of the Church gives us a useful tool for this very difficult and subtle task in cross-cultural ministry. The challenge which confronts the church in the United States today is how to develop a variety of different ethnic churches which are faithful to the church's doctrinal heritage and yet appropriate vehicles for successfully ministering to people of cultures different from ours. This has been a problem foreign missionaries have struggled with for years. Now the struggle has come home. In some ways, struggling with this problem in a multi-ethnic United States is going to be more difficult and subtle than it was in the foreign mission field. Rather than dealing with a single, relatively stable, culture, we must deal with many cultures in the process of changing as they adapt to life in this country. To prepare ourselves for the task ahead, we need to have an understanding of the profound relationship between religion and culture.

RELIGION AND CULTURE

Many of the new ethnic groups in the United States today represent cultures which have not been significantly

influenced by Christianity. As we seek to proclaim Christ
effectively to such people we need to investigate closely their
spiritual traditions since those are the traditions we seek to
change. The purpose of a culture's religion is "to define
origin, meaning and destiny"[9] for its people. As such, religion
profoundly shapes how people understand and relate to the
great questions of life and death. Religion is also one of the
chief ways in which a culture expresses its values and
celebrates its heroes while reinforcing its taboos and
condemning its villains. This is why the study of the religion
of a culture will help us understand why it developed many of
its social structures and ethical rules.

Charles Kraft reminds us that religion has both a
vertical function as it relates people to God and a horizontal
function as it relates people to each other and to their
surroundings. Because of these two functions, we must
closely study non-Christian religions, not merely dismiss them
as pagan. A non-Christian religion may provide "extremely
important horizontal functions"[10] even if it fails, by Christian
standards, to fulfill "the necessary vertical functions."[11] While
some of the horizontal functions of a non-Christian religion
may be antithetical to Christianity, most of them can be
performed by Christianity better than any other religion. This
will give power to our witness. If we create an expression of
Christianity which fails to address the horizontal functions
which a culture expects of a religion, our message will be
seen as defective.

Even the vertical functions of a culture's non-Christian
religion need to be investigated for they tell us much about
the religious images and attitudes of the people of that
culture. We should "not take for granted that images of God,
and the complex of attitudes deemed appropriate for
approaching God, are exactly the same in every culture . . . .
In different cultures, systems of worship and liturgy, of
preaching and of practice, subtly build up quite distinctive

languages of the soul."[12] While we would reject as false many of the theological teachings of a culture's non-Christian religion, we need to learn that culture's "language of the soul" if we hope to be successful in having them understand and accept, at a deep level, the unique message of the Gospel. Having understood the spiritual traditions of a culture, we can then proceed to the difficult task of creating a presence in that culture which is both relevant and Christian.

WHAT MAY CHANGE AND WHAT MUST REMAIN THE SAME?

There are two dangers as we seek to create a Christian presence in other cultures. The first is that in trying to relate our faith to another culture we make so many compromises that we, in fact, destroy the faith we seek to proclaim. A decision to allow Chinese to worship their ancestors and to accept this worship as obedience to the fourth commandment's requirement to "honor your father and mother," would be an example of this kind of destructive compromise.

A second danger is that we insist that people of other cultures accept and express the totality of the denomination wrapped in our own cultural package before we accept them as fellow members. This would mean that we consider every part of our experience, from our doctrine and our worship forms to our church polity and preferred architectural forms, as mandatory for all. Such an attitude would prevent us from seriously attempting to find the most culturally appropriate ways to develop an ethnic church. A decision to require all ethnic churches to use translations of Anglo hymnals as their only source of liturgy and hymns would be an example of succumbing to this danger.

The concept of cultural integration as expressed in the "Body of Christ" picture of the church can guide us safely between the extreme softness of too much compromise and the extreme rigidity of too little cultural awareness. Since we recognize that in the Church there is a unifying factor which must not change and a diversity factor which celebrates change, the thorny question is this: As you transfer the church from Anglo-American culture to another culture, what must stay the same and what may be changed? The following illustration is an attempt to begin to answer this question.

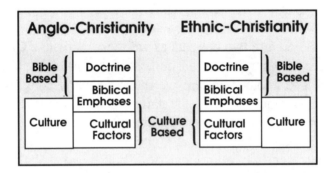

There are two parts to every expression of Christianity, the culture–based and the Bible–based. *Culture–based* refers to those factors which are based on the cultural distinctives of the people who are served by a particular church. Scripture neither mandates nor prohibits these factors. They are there to help facilitate the mission of the church, which is to disciple all peoples. By putting the Christian message in a culturally appropriate context, we have tried to be as effective as possible in fulfilling the Great Commission. To ignore culture as we structure the church's ministry would be a terrible mistake. The Anglo Lutheran church, for example, is an expression of Christianity which is admirably in tune with northern European culture and a large part of Anglo-American culture. This cultural sensitivity has helped the Lutheran Church to have a strong effect on the spiritual lives of people with an affinity for northern European culture.

Bible-based refers to those factors which are based on Scripture. There are two kinds of Bible-based factors. First, there is the doctrinal content which explains how a church interprets the message of Scripture. Second, there are those biblical emphases which help us illustrate Christian doctrine and which resonate particularly well in our culture. Each cultural expression of Christianity has its favorite Bible stories and Bible passages which sum up doctrinal concepts in ways that are particularly powerful to that culture. For example, we know that in early Christianity the biblical material concerning the birth of Jesus was not the object of nearly as much interest as it is today and Easter, not Christmas, was the major Christian holiday. During the Christmas season, we make much of the divinity and humanity of Christ. We see the Christmas story as a powerful illustration of his human and divine natures. The early Christians also believed in the divinity and humanity of Christ but they centered on other biblical stories and passages to illustrate this doctrine. Two contemporary illustrations come to mind. Black churches, as they relate to the freedom God offers his people, tend to focus on themes from the Exodus experience of Israel more than Anglo churches. Early in their history in America, Vietnamese Christians centered on themes from Israel's Exile in Babylon, especially Jeremiah's letter to the exiles in Jeremiah 29:4-14, as they struggled to come to terms with how they as refugees should relate to the larger American society. Anglo churches rarely study those same themes as they relate to the larger society.

When the Anglo church seeks to establish a presence in a new culture, it must tackle an important and sensitive question. Which aspects of the denomination must remain the same in any culture, and which parts may change? First, it is obvious that doctrine remains the same regardless of which culture the church attempts to reach. Second, while we would share with those of other cultures the biblical emphases which have been particularly important to us, we must remember that they may find other biblical emphases which illustrate doctrines for them better than the ones we use. Because of their unique "cultural eyes" they may perceive in certain Bible stories dimensions of our doctrinal heritage which we have not yet discovered. Therefore biblical emphases may change as a church moves from one culture to another. Third, the culture–based factors will almost surely change as the American church establishes its identity in other cultures. To insist that the culture–based factors in Anglo-American Christianity are mandatory for Christians of every culture would be a tragic mistake which would put enormous obstacles before us as we attempt to proclaim the Gospel in various cultures. We might experience some success, but our presence in the new ethnic communities would be marginal at best. As the Christian Church moves into new cultures, we must realize that such Anglo-American culture-based factors as liturgy, hymnody, Christian education, church architecture and church polity will undergo changes. This is a delicate task, for there is little broad-based agreement as to what the culture–based factors in the church are. Extremely monocultural churches are ill-prepared for this task. The principle of "one who knows but one culture, knows no culture"[13] can keep us from being sensitive to the areas of Anglo Christianity which are cultural. It can also be somewhat threatening to Anglos, for many of them fear that in changing the culture–based factors, violence might be done to the doctrine–based factors. As difficult as it may be, the task of creating new cultural expressions of Christianity is the key to successful ethnic ministry.

DONALD MCGAVRAN ON NEGOTIABLES
AND NON-NEGOTIABLES

Donald McGavran has some valuable insights on this subject.[14] He asserts that it is overly vague to speak about Christianity in general and culture in general when referring to the adjustments which may or may not be made in cross-cultural ministry. First, he addresses how we view culture. He suggests that we speak of "cultural components." "Culture comprises tens of thousands of components . . . . Only a few cultural components concern religious beliefs and practices . . . . Most components can be changed or even abandoned without trauma . . . . Christianity is wholly neutral to the vast majority of cultural components."[15] What about those components which deal with the spiritual dimension of life? They "fall into three categories . . . . Some components Christianity welcomes . . . . Some components Christianity changes or improves . . . . Some components Christianity declares are unacceptable to God and must be abandoned."[16]

Having divided the spiritual components of culture into three categories, McGavran divides Christianity into four categories. First is theological Christianity, or as he calls it, "Christianity one." This level of Christianity deals with "beliefs concerning God, man, sin, Scripture, salvation, eternal life, and right and wrong. Christians necessarily hold these on the basis of the authoritative biblical revelation and the institutional forms of the Church which the Bible requires and the New Testament displays as the apostolic model."[17] Here there is no room for negotiation. This is the supracultural dimension of Christianity and is normative for all peoples. Because it is supracultural, theological Christianity "constantly reviews all components of each culture and seeks to bring them into harmony with God's revealed will."[18] This corresponds to the changeless doctrinal message of the church. Second is ethical Christianity, which McGavran calls "Christianity two." It "is comprised of applied values systems—actions which Christians 'ought-to-do-under-various circumstances'."[19] Here there is limited room for negotiation. Great care must be taken, however, so that a change allowed here does not contradict a non-negotiable biblical teaching. Christianity one and two are closely connected. An example of that connection is the biblical mandate to "honor your father and your mother." That mandate is part of Christianity one and hence is binding on all cultures. The exact forms in which that honor is rendered may change from culture to culture. However, no form of rendering honor to the parents is permitted which would violate any clear teaching of Scripture. Third is denominational customs, or "Christianity three", which includes "ways of worship, forms of prayer, canons of song and praise, styles of architecture, and kinds of organizations."[20] Here there is wide room for negotiation, for few denominational customs are biblically mandated. Fourth are "the local customs of Christians"[21] or "Christianity four." This includes such things as "ways of earning a living, dressing, cutting the hair, eating, and going about the business of life."[22] Here we find the greatest opportunity for negotiation and the place where Christianity "accomodates itself most completely to local customs."[23]

Making needed adjustments without compromising the biblical message is still a difficult task. Sometimes, needed adjustments are not made and uniformity is demanded by the church where it is not demanded by the Bible. Other times adjustments are made which compromise Christianity in critical areas. Is there any corrective device which will help lead the church back to the truth once it has fallen victim to either of these errors? McGavran's answer is yes, and he points to a high view of Scripture as that corrective. Whatever errors are made in this complicated task "will be righted if the Bible is believed and taught as the infallible, inspired Word of God. The Holy Spirit will overrule [all human errors] and guide dedicated Christians into all truth."[24] McGavran's categories of Christianity and how they relate to what must remain the same and what may change as Christianity moves into new cultures addresses the same issue as the illustration above.

CONTEXTUALIZATION

As the church approaches this task, it would be helpful to utilize some of the concepts of the current debate over what many call "contextualization." Contextualization deals with communicating the biblical message across cultures in ways which are biblically accurate and culturally relevant. Though the term is relatively new, the concept is very old. In Acts 15, the first Church Council struggled with contextualization. It addressed the question of how much of the Jewish cultural framework needed to accompany the presentation of the Gospel to the Gentiles. Paul had to face the same question as he became the preeminent missionary to the Gentile world. His basic challenge was this: Jesus accomplished his work of salvation in a Jewish religious and cultural context. His ministry was the capstone of over two thousand years of Jewish history and messianic hope. The Gentile world had little interest in Jewish history and no sense of messianic hope. How then could the authentic Gospel be proclaimed with power and effectiveness in a non-Jewish context? Paul's answer was to take the Gospel message out of its Jewish cultural (but *not* its biblical or theological) context and connect it with the Greco-Roman context of his day. He laid out his basic philosophy in 1 Corinthians 9:19-23. He identified as much as possible with each group he approached, but he did not compromise the Gospel. Acts 17:16-34 gives a practical example of how Paul strove to make his message relevant to his hearers and faithful to his Lord. He had not yet written 1 Corinthians, but the philosophy he expressed there was already guiding him in Athens. When he addressed the meeting of the Areopagus, he contextualized the Gospel for the benefit of the philosophers who made up most of his audience. Beginning with what seemed like a compliment to the city for its paganism, Paul proceeded with a resurrection–centered message which used two direct quotes from Greek philosophers, along with a variety of allusions to literature familiar to his audience. It was the Gospel contextualized.

In today's world, all Gospel proclamation is cross–cultural communication. "The problem becomes how to understand and apply scriptural meanings presented in the forms of particular ancient cultures to the lives of contemporary peoples immersed in other cultures."[25] Contextualization is as important to communicating the Gospel to contemporary Anglos as it is to communicating it to any other group. The basic presupposition of those who seek to contextualize Christianity is that it "must be true to the complete authority and unadulterated message of the Bible on the one hand, and it must be related to the cultural, linquistic, and religious background of the respondents on the other."[26]

Here are some samples of the ongoing discussion of contextualization. The late African theologian Byang H. Kato challenged the church to maintain its commitment to the authority of Scripture as it struggled with the most appropriate ways to minister to the many cultures of Africa. He stressed this as he challenged those who would make culture, not Scripture, the fixed point in cross–cultural communication. José Miguez-Bonino expresses similar concerns as he critiques liberation theology. While maintaining a commitment to a socially active Christianity, he challenges the liberation theologians to make Scripture, not the political and social struggles of their countries, the fixed point in proclaiming and living the Gospel. Charles Kraft challenges the church to rethink its understanding of the cultural and supra-cultural in

Scripture and in our world today. He wants the church to be sensitive to its own cultural presuppositions, to have increased respect for "general revelation", that is God's extra-biblical revelation of himself, to appreciate fully the profound yet often subtle connection between culture and communication, and to be open to new ways of expressing the biblical message in the various cultures of our world. There are many others who are making valuable contributions to the current discussion of contextualization.

The central subject of contextualization is the proper separation of the changeless and the changing in the proclamation of the biblical message. Because of this, the contextualization debate struggles with the same basic question the church faces as it decides what must remain the same and what may change in the various ethnic expressions of Christianity. We need biblical scholars to study the contextualization debate carefully, for it may well produce principles which we can use to develop a church which is both truly multi-ethnic and truly Christian.

The following is an example, taken from my own denomination, of how contextualization can help in this task. In the Lutheran church there is a continuing and emotional debate over our traditional worship forms. On the one side are those who see our way of worship as a highly contextualized presentation of our doctrine. They see it as being profoundly shaped by northern European culture. They assert that it is necessary, in today's culturally diverse world, to separate the cultural from the Scriptural, the changing from the changeless, in traditional Lutheran worship. Only after this is done, they say, can we develop worship forms which are useful in other cultures. They are so fearful of forcing northern European culture on non-European ethnics that they discount all traditional Lutheran worship forms. On the other side of the debate are those who regard traditional Lutheran worship forms as based almost entirely on biblical truth and the apostolic Christian experience. They acknowledge very little European cultural influence in traditional Lutheran worship forms. They are so fearful that doctrinal error might accompany liturgical change that they resist any change in worship forms. They would have all ethnic groups accept, with only minor adaptations, traditional Lutheran worship forms as a part of our doctrinal heritage. The insights provided by contextualization may well lead both sides to a deeper appreciation of the doctrinal and cultural components of worship.

This delicate balance between the changeless and the changing brings us back to the concept of cultural integration as expressed in the Body of Christ picture of the church. We previously looked at this picture in relation to ethnicity in the church. There, Christ was the unifying factor and ethnic identity was the diversity factor. When we apply this picture to the task of creating a new cultural expression for the church, we can again use the idea of unity and diversity. The head of the body represents the changeless, non-negotiable, supra-cultural, Bible–based Christian doctrine. Utilizing McGavran's terms, the head is Christianity one, or theological Christianity. This doctrinal dimension controls everything any Christian church in any culture says and does. It corresponds to the ideological commitment layer in American identity. The body represents the changing, culture-based factors of the church and the unique biblical emphases which will be developed by each culture. This corresponds to McGavran's Christianity two, three and four. Here is where the church makes the adjustments necessary to become culturally relevant to the people it seeks to reach. While this doesn't solve all the problems, it does give us a tool with which to address them. If a church decides a factor belongs to the head, it will decide that the factor under consideration cannot be changed and must be adopted as is from the Anglo-

American church. If it decides a factor properly belongs to the body, it will allow freedom and creativity in that area.

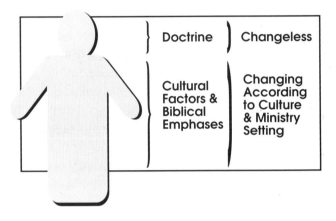

At present, we have no well articulated, culturally sensitive set of principles to guide us. The debate about what may and may not change in the church as it faces a changing world has been filled with emotion and hidden agendas and has, thus far, produced more heat than light. The debate has been shaped more by how people relate to the general subject of change in the church than by sound biblical theology and informed cultural sensitivity. We must now move to a new level in this debate, a level which brings together careful biblical scholarship and a deep understanding of the latest insights of the social sciences and ethnic studies. They must be brought together—not in combat, but in service to the Great Commission.

DISCUSSION QUESTIONS
1.   Define and discuss the three layers of American identity.

2. Discuss the relationship between ethnic identity and shared American history. How do you, personally, relate to these two dimensions of your American identity?

3. Seven ways of dealing with ethnic identity were defined in this chapter. They were: Americanization, assimilation, acculturation, toleration, cultural integration, cultural pluralism, and cultural separatism. Which one most nearly describes your attitude toward ethnicity? Which one most nearly describes your church's attitude? Which one, do you think, most nearly describes the attitude of recently arrived ethnic groups?

4. What relationship do you see between the concept of cultural integration and the biblical teaching of the Church as the Body of Christ?

5. Which of the five models for cross-cultural ministry on the local level would be most appropriate in your situation, considering your congregation and community?

6. What do you think your denomination should be doing about ethnic ministry on the regional and national levels? How would you be willing to help it accomplish these things?

7. Discuss the relationship between religion and culture and how this influences cross-cultural ministry?

8. Is the Great Commission more method oriented (that is, mainly concerned with *how* we evangelize) or results oriented (that is, mainly interested in "making

disciples of all nations")? Are you, your congregation, and your denomination more interested in methods or results?

9.   Discuss the relationship between Bible-based factors and culture-based factors in your denomination. How willing is your denomination to allow change in the culture-based factors? How willing are you and your congregation?

10.   How can Donald McGavran's insights regarding negotiables and non-negotiables be helpful in answering the question of what changes and what remains the same as your congregation or denomination moves into ministry with a new ethnic group?

11.   Why is it necessary to contextualize the Gospel? Give some examples of how your denomination has contextualized the Gospel for your benefit. How important is it for your denomination to re-contextualize the Gospel for each new group it seeks to reach?

5

MINISTRY IMPLICATIONS OF THE CULTURAL INTEGRATION MODEL OF THE CHURCH

The cultural integration model of the church celebrates the cultural uniqueness of all the ethnic groups which make up our nation and our denomination. In order to celebrate cultural uniqueness, we must understand the uniqueness of the cultures which surround us. This means we must invest time, energy, and money in projects which carefully study the various cultures to which we wish to minister. In doing this, we can find appropriate ways to maintain the unity of the faith while affirming the diversity of God's people.

The church has three valuable resources at its disposal as it lays the intellectual framework for cross-cultural ministry. We should treasure our people who have experience in foreign mission fields. They have much practical knowledge about establishing a Christian presence in new cultures. Because of the many cultures which interrelate with each other in the United States, the current home mission front is more culturally complex than most foreign mission fields, but our foreign mission personnel still have many valuable lessons to teach us. We should treasure those in our denomination who are skilled in the disciplines of sociology and anthropology. They have the ability to describe accurately the cultural distinctives of various groups. This will help us understand the uniqueness of those we intend to reach with the Gospel. We should treasure those in our denomination who represent various ethnic groups. We should listen to them and let them teach us how we can best minister to their people. If some of their suggestions disturb us, we should remember that the cause may be our cultural insensitivity, not the inappropriateness of their suggestions. We will have to study and listen like never before as we prepare to create a truly multi-cultural denomination. This intellectual dimension is not a panacea for all the challenges of cross-cultural ministry, but without it we cannot even make a fruitful beginning.

MINISTRY IMPLICATIONS OF UNCONSCIOUS CULTURE

In the second chapter of this book, the concept of unconscious culture was defined. This concept demonstrates why understanding a culture's distinctives does not automatically give us the tools to minister to it. We can study and listen with all our resources and, in certain ways, still be outsiders when it comes to ministering across cultural lines. Unconscious culture refers to the basic assumptions and organizing principles which give a culture its uniqueness but are not consciously understood by the people of the culture. Even if a person from one culture learns the unconscious distinctives of another culture, they can rarely be internalized so they shape him or her the way they shape people who were raised in that culture.

In view of this, we need to recruit and train candidates for the ministry from the various ethnic groups we want to reach with the Gospel. Teaching Anglo-Americans how to speak Spanish, for example, will never be the most effective way to reach the many Hispanic groups in the United States today. Even after mastering Spanish and learning the conscious culture of a particular Hispanic group, the Anglo-American will probably never internalize the group's unconscious culture and thus will always, to some degree, be an outsider to that group. This doesn't mean we cannot use Anglo-Americans in ministry to non-Anglo groups. This may be the best we can do, in some cases, for the present, but our goal should always be a ministry for ethnics, by ethnics. This is a principle we should remember as we consider the future shape of ministry among the African-Americans, which also is cross-cultural ministry in ways many Anglos fail to realize.

VARIATIONS WITHIN MAJOR CULTURAL GROUPS

We also need to realize that major ethnic groups are complex and contain many sub-groups which have their own cultural distinctives. Hispanic, for example, is a name we give to a group of groups. It refers to Mexicans, Salvadorans, Nicaraguans and Cubans, to name only a few. While all of the groups speak Spanish, not even the language situation is as simple as one might think. Each group has given its own "spin" to the Spanish language, which means that knowing Mexican Spanish is not exactly the same as knowing Cuban Spanish. While all Hispanics share certain conscious and unconscious cultural distinctives, each of the groups also has a unique set of distinctives. It would be wrong to assume that a Mexican could be a naturally effective minister to Nicaraguans or Cubans simply because he spoke Mexican Spanish and shared some of the cultural distinctives of these groups. It would also be wrong to assume that strategies developed for reaching, say, Cubans, would be equally effective for all other Hispanic groups. Sensitivity to subtle variations within major groups will help us develop the most effective ministry strategies for each sub-group.

DEVELOPING MINISTRY RESOURCES

When it comes to developing resources for ethnic ministry we would be well advised to remember the principle of ministry for ethnics, by ethnics. The best people to prepare the ministry resources for an ethnic group are people from that group. They should not be asked simply to translate Anglo-American English resources into their language. They should be given the freedom to create resources which are culturally appropriate for them. If this is not possible, then at least there should be a group of ethnics which can give feedback and creative suggestions as others develop the resources. We also need to pay attention to the art work which accompanies our resources. Visual communication is powerful and should reflect the racial composition and cultural uniqueness of the target audience.

MINISTRY IMPLICATIONS OF
LOW AND HIGH CULTURAL CONTEXT

As we seek to minister appropriately to other cultures we need to remember the low context—high context continuum introduced in chapter two. Most mainline, traditional denominations in this country tend to be rather low context expressions of Christianity. Our high emphasis on doctrine and our generally shallow commitment to fellowship, our love of the intellectual dimension of life and our fear of the emotional dimension, our commitment to pre-written liturgies and our suspicion of the spontaneous in our worship life, our way of filling pastoral vacancies in local congregations, our highly organized church government and the way we shape agendas at our meetings, all present problems when we move into ministry with high context cultures. It is interesting that the fastest growing American–based church bodies in high context cultures are usually representatives of the charismatic movement, a movement which tends to be a rather high context expression of Christianity. To be successful in cross-cultural ministry among high context ethnic groups (and most of the new ethnic groups in the United States are high context), we must develop a high context expression of Christianity. This kind of Christianity would blend the doctrinal depth we wish to maintain with the emotional depth necessary to communicate effectively to high context cultures. If we do not rise to this challenge, we will be relegated to the fringes of these new ethnic communities.

In interpersonal relationships with the new ethnics, Anglos need to remember the context factor. Being low context, Anglos invest minimal time and energy developing personal relationships with most of their fellow workers. People from most of the new ethnic groups in the United States will find it difficult to work together with Anglos and trust them unless Anglos are willing to spend more time than is their custom in building relationships. Anglos need to adjust upward their cultural context if they want the best working relationships with the new ethnics in this country. An Asian friend of mine voiced a frustration born of the context gap between Anglos and ethnics. He said of an Anglo coworker, "The only time he ever invites me to go to lunch with him is when he wants something from me." That reality was causing strains in their relationship.

MINISTRY IMPLICATIONS OF MONOCHRONIC AND POLYCHRONIC TIME

Most of the new ethnic groups in the United States today come from cultures which are not only high context but also polychronic. Anglos, however, tend to be profoundly monochronic.

We are highly concerned about when things begin and end, scheduling a time for everything, and adhering strictly to our schedule. We value human relationships, but we tend to become frustrated when the requirments of a relationship interfere with our well-planned schedules. Any Anglo pastor whose Sunday service runs longer than an hour and a half can see in the pained faces of his parishoners how monochronic we are! Polychronic people do not share our passion for scheduling. Their passion is for quality human relationships. When polychronic and monochronic people attempt to work together and do cooperative future planning, there can be tension and misunderstanding. Monochronic Anglos will tend to become frustrated with polychronic ethnics and to regard them as lazy, unreliable, and unable to make specific plans for the future. Polychronic ethnics will tend to become frustrated with monochronic Anglos and to regard them as overly aggressive, emotionally shallow, and unduly concerned about the future. With a cultural integration mindset, however, these difficulties can be managed. This mindset approaches other cultures with an openness to learn and appreciate other ways of seeing life. Anglo-Americans can learn some enriching lessons from people who value events over schedules and interpersonal relationships over clocks. The ethnics, for their part, can learn to understand that within the context of mainstream American culture there are sound reasons for timeliness and specific future planning. As both groups approach each other in this spirit, many difficulties will be avoided—or at least lessened.

THE DANGER OF CULTURAL PROJECTION

The stresses and strains of working together with people from another culture can lead to cultural projection. In cultural projection, the rules for judging behavior in one culture are used to judge the behavior of people from another culture. I have heard Anglos condemn Koreans because "they don't know how to discipline their children," Chinese because "they're pushy and stand too close to you," Mexicans because "they're always late," and African-Americans because "they don't know how to speak good English." Each comment was an exercise in cultural projection. If we are to evaluate properly the behavior of people from another culture we must use the rules for evaluation which apply to that culture. Then and only then will our positive or negative evaluations have any validity. The cultural integration mindset will help us avoid this pitfall. It affirms a sensitivity which would never use the rules of one culture to judge another culture or the behavior of its people.

CONFLICT RESOLUTION

Despite our best Christian efforts, there will be times when conflict arises and begins to escalate in cross-cultural ministry. Every culture develops its own rules and structures when it comes to conflict escalation. If I make you angry, I need to know two things. First, I need to know that you are angry, and second, I need to know how angry you are. As I continue to relate to you, I need to know whether you're getting more upset, which means the conflict is escalating, or less upset, which means the conflict is being resolved. Anglo-American culture has developed a language of conflict escalation which allows me to know, though not always with complete accuracy, how tense a situation is and whether we are heading toward an explosion of violence or a peaceful resolution. Edward T. Hall describes the Anglo-American language of conflict escalation in this way: "For those of us who come from the northern European tradition, disputes escalate in stages, starting with nonverbal cues and body messages and proceeding to indirection, verbal hints, verbal confrontation, legal action, and finally force, or physical action."[1]

Other cultures have developed different languages of conflict escalation. The reason cross-cultural conflicts are so hard to resolve is that neither group understands the other's language of conflict escalation. For this reason, neither group is sure how major or minor the conflict is, whether it is escalating or de-escalating, or which words and/or actions might be appropriate in the situation. Hall describes the difficulties which can arise when people fail to understand the subtleties of conflict escalation in a cross-cultural situation. "In face-to-face relations in Japan, amenities and cordialities are maintained, no matter how one is feeling. To show one's anger is tantamount to admitting loss of control (and face), unless, of course, *things have gone too far.*' There are no adumbrative signs to warn of impending disaster, and Americans, as well as many Europeans, will unconsciously push and push—looking for structure, pattern, and limits. Because they are unfamiliar with the Japanese system, Europeans are almost inevitably destined to go too far."[2]

Another example of how different cultures devise different ways of dealing with conflicts involves the point at which a conflict between two individuals or groups needs an outside counselor. In Anglo-American culture, conflicts are usually resolved with "one-to-one direct address, confrontation, self–disclosure, negotiation and resolution."[3] If an outside third party is brought in, it signals a high degreee of tension and an admission that one or both parties have failed to deal adequately with the situation. In many non-Anglo cultures, however, "conflicts are immediately referred to a third party—an older, wiser, neutral, skilled family member or a trusted person from the community."[4] Thus, utilizing the services of a third party to resolve a conflict is regarded as a first response, not a last resort. From this, it is evident that even the suggestion to call in a third party to mediate a dispute can mean quite different things to different groups.

Conflict can tear churches apart. It is difficult enough to keep conflicts from doing damage in a church where all share the same culture and understand, to some degree at least, their common language of conflict escalation. When individuals, groups or churches attempt to resolve conflicts in cross-cultural situations, special care must be taken. Each group must attempt to learn at least some of the other group's language of conflict resolution. In addition, if a conflict arises, each group must honestly interpret for the other how they are feeling and where this conflict is leading in terms of words and actions. Properly handling cross–cultural conflicts is important enough for the church to give some major consideration to this topic as it moves into cross-cultural ministry.

INTERPATHIC CROSS-CULTURAL COUNSELORS
FOR THE CHURCH

Since cross–cultural ministry can involve many situations in which conflict can arise, the church should utilize the talents of people who David Augsburger, in his book *Pastoral Counseling*

Across Cultures, calls "interpathic" counselors. He defines interpathy as "an intentional cognitive envisioning and affective experiencing of another's thoughts and feelings, even though the thoughts rise from another process of knowing, the values grow from another frame of moral reasoning, and the feelings spring from another basis of assumptions. In interpathic caring, the process of 'feeling with' and 'thinking with' another requires that one enter the other's world of assumptions, beliefs, and values and temporarily take them as one's own."[5] Putting aside his own cultural frame of reference, the interpathic counselor "believe(s) what the other believes, see(s) as the other sees, value(s) what the other values, and feel(s) the consequent feelings as the other feels them."[6] He then applies this to reaching out to people from another culture. "I, the culturally different, seek to learn and fully entertain with my consciousness a foreign belief. I take a foreign perspective, base my thought on a foreign assumption, and allow myself to feel the resultant feelings and their congitive and emotive consequences."[7]

As the church seeks to reach out effectively to the many cultures in the United States today, it needs to identify and utilize the unique gifts of the people to whom Augsburger was referring. We need to find and utilize our modern day "Pauls" who can fully enter into other cultures for the sake of the Gospel while retaining their identity with and sensitivity to their own culture. While some of these people will have missionary backgrounds, others will not. Openness and sensitivity to those who are different, who are struggling and who are outcasts, linked to a strong sense of self-identity, is more important for interpathy than any specific background of experience. These people would not enter a culture with the idea of doing direct mission work. They would function as interpathic cross-cultural counselors for the church. They would perform two valuable services. First, they would help mediate cross-cultural conflict on the local, regional, and national levels. Second, they would help create cultural sensitivity among the various ethnic groups in the denomination. For example, they would use their interpathic cross-cultural gifts to help guide the Anglo church as it seeks to create a multicultural denomination which accurately reflects the New Testament model of the Body of

Christ. At the same time, they would sensitize the non-Anglo cultures in the United States to the struggles of the Anglo church as it seeks to become truly multicultural.

ETHNICITY AND PERSONAL CHOICE

In the cultural integration model of the church, we are careful not to force people to give up their ethnic identity and become like Anglo-Americans because, after all, they are in the United States now. We recognize and affirm the unique identity of each person, even if that identity makes him very different from us in certain ways. At the same time, we should avoid the mistake of forcing people into ethnic molds because of their backgrounds. A Chinese-American, for example, has the freedom to assimilate completely into Anglo-American culture if he wishes. We are not ideologically opposed to assimilation. We are concerned that it be a freely chosen path and not a forced march. No one should be a slave of ethnic identity or assimilationist pressures.

John Higham, in describing his vision of multi-ethnic America, which he calls "pluralistic integration," says that pluralistic integration

> will not eliminate ethnic boundaries. But neither will it maintain them intact. It will uphold the validity of a common culture, to which all individuals have access, while sustaining the efforts of minorities to preserve and enhance their own integrity. In principle, this dual commitment can be met by distinquishing between boundaries and nucleus. No ethnic group under these terms may have the support of the general community in strengthening its boundaries. All boundaries are understood to be permeable. Ethnic nuclei, on the other hand, are respected as enduring centers of social action. If self–preservation requires, they may claim exemption from certain universal rules, as the Amish now do from the school laws in some states. Both integration and ethnic cohesion are recognized as worthy goals, which different individuals will accept in different degrees. Ethnicity varies enormously in intensity from one person to another."[8]

Nathan Glazer points out that one of the aspects of ethnic

patterns in this country which both frees us and confuses us is that "in the United States, one is required neither to put on ethnicity nor to take it off."[9] Thus there are no firm rules for how ethnic any person, group or church must be. With no firm rules, we must approach each person and group with a sensitivity as to which choices they wish to make. We do not judge those choices; we respond to them. We must also choose which models of ministry and church development we will utilize, depending on the ethnic intensity of the people we hope to reach. The purpose of the Christian church is not to dictate ethnic consciousness but to proclaim the Gospel of Jesus Christ and make disciples of all nations.

We have now returned to the basic purpose of this book, which is to help us fulfill the Great Commission in multi-ethnic America. All of the anthropological, sociological, historical, biblical, and practical insights in this book are meaningless unless we utilize them to reach people with the saving Gospel of Jesus Christ. Some may want to take issue with certain ideas and suggestions contained in this book. That is fine. This book is not an attempt to speak the final word about the shape of cross–cultural ministry in the church. It is an attempt to begin the discussion. Some of the best ideas and suggestions are still to be expressed. But as we discuss the issues, let us remember that we are not playing intellectual games here. We are dealing with the eternal destinies of the people of our own nation. Some may say "yea and amen" to what they have read and then go on with business as usual. This book was not written so that people would agree with its contents. It was written as a tool for cross–cultural evangelism. Tools are not made for approval but for work. If you agree with the cultural integration model of the church, then let's get to work and make that model a living reality!

The coming decades are crucial for the church as it addresses the ethnic diversity of urban America. "Playing it

safe" will be the sure road to disaster. "Business as usual"
will mean we will soon be out of business in many of our
nation's great urban areas. We must take some risks and dare
to fail. As people of faith who believe in the healing of
forgiveness we should be willing to take those risks. The
greatest tragedy is *not* failing in some project or speaking an
idea which we later must retract. The greatest tragedy is
failing to speak the Good News of salvation through Christ,
powerfully and effectively, to all of the peoples who make up
this great nation. God has given this generation of American
Christians a unique mission opportunity. Never before has
such an opportunity confronted us. If we fail to respond, it
will soon pass us by. In John 4:35, Jesus says to his disciples,
"Open your eyes and look at the fields! They are ripe for
harvest." They were then. They are now. But the harvest
opportunity will not last forever. Let's move ahead, now!

DISCUSSION QUESTIONS

1.   It was stated in this chapter that in light of the
influence of unconscious culture, our goal should be
"ministry for ethnics by ethnics." How do you react
to that?

2.   What kind of ethnic ministry resources do you need to
minister to the ethnic groups in your community? Are
those resources available to you? If not, what can you
do to see to it that they become available?

3.   Where do your denomination and congregation fit into
the low-context/high-context continuum? Where do the
ethnic groups in your community fit into that
continuum? What does this mean for you and them as
you move into ministry with these groups?

4. Where do your denomination and congregation fit into the monochronic/polychronic time continuum? Where do the ethnic groups in your community fit into that continuum? What does this mean for you and them as you move into ministry with these groups?

5. Do you know of any examples where conflict became destructive in a cross-cultural ministry situation? What kind of safeguards would you like to see established in your ministry situation so that cross-cultural conflict can be managed in a positive way?

6. This chapter asserts that "the purpose of the Christian church is not to dictate ethnic consciousness but to proclaim the Gospel of Jesus Christ and make disciples of all nations." How will this concept influence your ministry to the ethnic groups in your community? How will it influence your relationships with individuals from those groups?

7. Are you ready to reach out in ministry to people from another culture? Why? Why not?

8. What other individuals and groups might benefit from the insights contained in this book?

GLOSSARY

Acculturation: The primary and most commonly understood meaning is an individual's learning the rules of and coming to terms with a new culture. A secondary meaning, and that is the one which predominates in this book, is that acculturation is an attitude held by those in the dominant Anglo-American culture which opposes any group's desire to maintain a high degree of public ethnic identity but which would allow for a certain amount of ethnicity displayed within the family or within the ethnic community. It is a definition of acculturation wherein some in the dominant culture attempt to dictate to those who are acculturating when, where, and to what degree ethnicity is allowed.

Americanization: An attitude which demands that ethnics completely shed their ethnicity before they can be accepted as true Americans. It opposes any cultural traditions not rooted in Anglo-Saxon culture and opposes the public use of any language other than English.

Americanization movement: Beginning around 1900, this movement sought to reduce ethnic consciousness to nothing more than a remembrance of ethnic origins. It especially opposed "hyphenation," that is, the practice of identifying oneself as German-American, Irish-American, etc.

Anglo-Saxon racialism: A movement begun in the early 1900s, which maintained that it could be scientifically proven that Anglo-Saxons were innately superior to all other cultural groups and that only they possessed the basic commitment to the political and personal virtues upon which the United States was founded.

Assimilation: An attitude which asks ethnics to shed their ethnicity for the harmonious function of society. It assumes that Anglo-American culture is superior to all other cultures and thus should replace a person's ethnic identity.

154

Conscious culture: Those elements of a person's culture of which he is consciously aware and which he can define and describe.

Contextualization: The study of how to communicate the Christian message in new cultures in ways which are biblically accurate and culturally relevant.

Cultural integration: An attitude which celebrates ethnic diversity and allows wide latitude for ethnic expression. It also asks ethnics to take seriously their commitment to the American ideals of liberty, equality, and democracy as that which gives unity to the country.

Cultural pluralism: An attitude which affirms that cultural distinctives should be preserved and celebrated while at the same time all should participate in a common national culture.

Cultural projection: Using the rules of one culture to interpret and pass judgment on the words, attitudes, and actions of people from a different culture.

Cultural relativism: The relative presence of good and evil, sin and grace, God and Satan in all cultures. Because of this, no one culture is perfect and therefore superior to all others.

Cultural separatism: An attitude which seeks to insulate ethnic groups from being changed by the general American culture, even to the point of geographic separation so that groups could express their uniqueness without compromise.

Culture: An interrelated system of thought, belief, morality, ethical principles, social and family structures, and physical products developed by a group in order to organize life in ways which are understandable and workable so that they can survive, attain their valued goals, and successfully adapt to change in their environment.

Ethnic boundaries: The degree of ethnicity a group expects of its members if they are to be considered part of the group.

Ethnic group: A group of people who share a common racial, regional, cultural, linguistic, and religious background.

Ethnic nuclei: Those organizations and social structures an ethnic group develops which help it to have continued access to its cultural heritage and which facilitate the practice of its cultural distinctives.

Ethnocentrism: An attitude that one's own group is the most important group, that its needs are centrally important, and that it represents the ultimate good.

High context culture: A culture which places a high value on interpersonal relationships and, because of this, requires a considerable amount of "getting to know" people before trust is extended, decisions are made, and business is transacted.

Immigration Act of 1965 (Hart-Cellar): Legislation which abolished the previous immigration quotas which were biased against Asia and Africa. This opened the U. S. to a significant influx of so-called "Third World" immigrants.

Intercultural education: A pre-World War II educational program which taught toleration of the religious, racial, and cultural differences of others.

Interpathy: The ability to enter into another cultural framework so completely that you can think the way people in that culture think, experience the world the way they experience it, believe what they believe, value what they value, and feel what they feel.

Low context culture: A culture which places a low value on interpersonal relationships and, as a result, requires only a minimum of "getting to know" people before trust is extended, decisions are made, and business is transacted.

Melting pot: The concept that in the United States all ethnic differences gradually disappear and a new American identity is forged.

Monochronic time: A view of time which stresses the precise scheduling of events and adhering to the schedule, promptness, and future planning.

Paternalism: A subtle form of racism.

Polychronic time: A view of time which stresses interpersonal relationships, pursuing an encounter to its natural completion rather than following a pre-planned time schedule, several things happening at once, and a greater concern for what is happening in the present than in planning for the future.

Prejudice: An attitude which belittles the importance and humanity of any group which differs from "our" group.

Racism: An attitude which actively seeks ways to humiliate, dominate, and control those who are the objects of prejudice.

Supra-cultural: The doctrinal part of Christianity which stands above all cultures and is normative in all cultures. That part of Christianity which remains the same as the church makes adjustments to minister cross-culturally.

Toleration: An attitude which accepts ethnic diversity as a fact of life. It does not celebrate it but permits it, since attempting to destroy ethnicity would do more harm to the general society than allowing it certain limited expressions.

Unconscious culture: The basic assumptions and organizing principles upon which the most profound distinctives of a culture rest, but which are not understood on a conscious level by those whose culture they shape.

Appendix A
GET READY . . .

(The pastor prepares himself for ethnic ministry)

1.   Begin with prayer and personal Bible study. This is a spiritual project, and time on your knees will be time well spent. To proceed without daily prayer is to deny your faith and invite failure. Your Bible study will be especially fruitful if you spend a considerable amount of time studying those sections of Scripture which deal with an evangelistic theme. There will be many details to attend to as you move toward ministry with another ethnic group. There will be frustrations, difficulties, and perhaps even some failures. At the very beginning, it is important to concentrate on the basic reason for entering into this ministry. You are reaching out toward another ethnic group in your community because, as a Christian, you live in the light of the Great Commission. Christ has given you a part in the work of winning the world to Himself. If you live in a community which is multicultural, you have a special challenge and opportunity with relation to the Great Commission. The challenge is to find a way to bridge the gaps which separate your ministry from the major ethnic groups in your community. The opportunity is to see people eternally changed by Jesus Christ as they are touched by a new ethnic ministry. In other words, the opportunity is to see the Great Commission fulfilled in ways that many others never will, because their communities lack the diversity of your community. So, in the midst of the difficulties of the task ahead, center your heart and the hearts of your fellow workers on the Great Commission dimension of this sharing relationship. The eternities of God-created, blood-bought human beings depend on the success of this endeavor. **Never lose sight of this important truth!**

2.   Do an analysis of your congregation. How many people can be served adequately by your facilities? If your congregation has remained constant in its membership or if it has

been decreasing in the past ten years, find out why this trend has emerged. If your congregation has been growing, you need to ask yourself if, in a few years, you might need all the available space in your facility for your congregation. The purpose of this analysis is twofold. First, you need to do everything possible to assure a solid future for your congregation. Plunging into cross-cultural ministry is no replacement for effectively shepherding your own flock. Second, you need to know if your facilities will be adequate to serve the needs of a new ministry. If not, a new ethnic ministry will need to be housed off-site.

      3.   Do a community analysis. Your public library will have demographic information on your community. Find out as much as you can about the current status of your community. What is the ethnic makeup right now? Also, take a look at trends which will affect the future. Which ethnic groups will be increasing, which will remain constant, and which will decline? If the information you find at the library is dated or insufficient, contact representatives of the major ethnic groups in your area and get their input. Another good place to get current information on population trends is from local public schools. This need not be a lengthy, detailed process. You're just testing the water to see if there is an increasing need for cross-cultural ministry in your area and which ethnic group or groups you should be thinking about.

      4.   Get to know representatives of the major ethnic groups in your area. Most ethnic groups have some sort of community organizations which are involved in the life of their people. Talk to the ethnic leaders and find out what's happening in their community. Go as a servant. Let them know that you are seeking guidance as to how you might best use your position as a pastor to serve the various groups in your community. They may make suggestions which fall outside your sphere of interest, but listen carefully to everything they say. Soak up all the information you can. It could also prove quite valuable for you to contact some ethnics who are not a part of the leadership of their communities. They might see things differently from the leaders, and their perspectives might give you new insights into what's really happening on the streets.

      5.   Keep up on the news which is coming from the

major ethnic groups in your area. Make a folder for one or more groups and keep a file of all the information you can get on each group.

6.   Decide which ethnic group you want to reach out to. Then you can concentrate on one group and not have to extend yourself in several different directions at the same time.

7.   Find ways in which you and your congregation can be of some service to the group you have chosen. This provides opportunities for both you and your people to get to know more about another culture.

8.   Read books which introduce you to the history and culture of the ethnic group. Your contacts in the ethnic community can steer you to good information.

9.   Familiarize yourself with their language—at least a little. This shows that you are truly interested in them. If you learn enough to extend greetings in their language, it will mean a lot to them.

10.   Try to contact people from the ethnic community who are interested in starting a new congregation. Perhaps in the beginning this will be just one person or family around which others from that culture can gather. The goal now is to gather a group of ethnics in your congregation which can become the core group of a new ethnic ministry. This individual or group can attend your services and some of your congregational activities, either occasionally or regularly. This will help the two groups begin to get acquainted with each other. The ongoing process of informing your congregation about this new group and sensitizing your congregation to these people as human beings and fellow members of the Body of Christ is important as you move toward ministry with them. This informing and sensitizing begins when your people make that first significant contact, within your church family, with an individual or family from another culture. You should spend the time and effort to make sure that this initial exposure is a positive experience for your congregation and for the ethnics. You will not attempt to assimilate this group into your congregation. From the beginning, they will be encouraged to develop a ministry which best enables them to reach others of their group. As this group grows, your people can begin to taste some of the excitement of seeing the

Great Commission fulfilled in another segment of their community. You can remind them that this is only the beginning of the great things that can happen in a church which is willing to let God lead it into a ministry relationship with another ethnic group.

Appendix B
. . . GET SET . . .

(Preparing the congregation)

Once a pastor has decided that God is calling him to lead his congregation into ministry with people from a different culture, he should begin to prepare his congregation for this new step of faith. Even as he prepares himself through the steps listed in Appendix A, he should be laying the groundwork in the congregation for ethnic ministry. Again, as in the personal preparation, there are several steps necessary to make sure the proper congregational preparation is done.

1.   Ask for God's direction. Preparing your congregation for ministry with people from a different culture is more difficult than preparing yourself for this relationship. Many different points of view are represented in any congregation, and you'll be dealing with everything from enthusiastic acceptance to extreme opposition. You'll need to ask God to guide both you and your congregation through the delicate times ahead so you can have a successful ethnic ministry.

2.   Share your vision of ethnic ministry with a small group in your congregation. There are several groups you might chose to work with. You might want to begin with your Church Council or Board of Directors. You might want to begin with the Board of Elders. You might want to ask your church leadership to appoint a special task force to evaluate the possibilities for ministry with another cultural group. You might want to keep the group informal. In this case, you would contact a few people in your church who may or may not be in official leadership positions and meet with them. This group should contain at least a few key congregational leaders. The basic concern is that you choose your first group carefully. First, you want to meet with people who you have reason to believe will react positively to your vision and will support your vision to the larger congregation. Second, you don't

want to create problems for yourself by appearing to bypass your congregational leadership. Only you, guided by God, will know which group you should begin with.

Meet several times with this group for sharing, Bible study, and prayer. The Bible study resources included in Appendix E and the Discussion Questions at the end of each chapter could be adapted and used with this group. As you prepared yourself for this new ministry, you focused on the Great Commission as the basic motivation for ethnic ministry. As you share the vision of this ministry with your congregation, you need to give them the same basic motivation. You don't want your congregation to move ahead with this project out of loyalty to you as a person, or because it needs extra money, or because it might impress other congregations. You want the support of your congregation based squarely on the Great Commission. So, as you share, study, and pray with this first group, make sure you start at the beginning. Ground them in the Great Commission vision and inspire them with Great Commission zeal. Then, their support for ethnic ministry will be Bible-based and will last through the difficult work ahead.

3.   If your first sharing group was not the Church Council or Board of Directors, this group should be your second sharing group. Share your vision with them, study the Bible with them, pray with them, and ask for their support. Again, the focus should be on how this ministry helps fulfill the Great Commission. Ideally, when all is said and done, your congregation should quote Matthew 28:19-20 when asked why they are doing ethnic ministry. They should not quote you. If you receive the support of your Church Council or Board of Directors, it should be the group which, along with you, prepares a brief statement on the mission of the church, the concept of ministry, and the stewardship of facilities which will lay the groundwork for the congregational phase of vision sharing. This entire document should be based on the Great Commission.

This group should also decide which of the five options listed on pages 120-121 is the most appropriate for your congregation and community. The material presented from this point on applies most directly to a church which has selected the "partner church" option. It can, however, be adapted for use in the local situation regardless of which option is chosen.

4.   Once you have secured the support of your congregational leadership to begin a new ethnic ministry, you should contact the regional officials of your denomination to let them know that your congregation is considering a sharing relationship with an ethnic church. (The assumption here, as throughout this section, is that you are moving toward a sharing relationship with an ethnic church of your denomination. If you intend to enter into a sharing relationship with an ethnic group outside your denomination, the material in Appendix D will speak to that issue.) They can tell you what plans for ethnic ministry they have in your area, and you can share with them the needs you have discovered. If they have plans to develop an ethnic church in your area, then you can offer your church as the site of this new ministry. If they have no plans in your area, share with them the information you gathered which convinced you of the need for such a ministry. You probably will not be able to move ahead with the development of an ethnic church without the financial support of the larger church. Work with them on this matter. Also, your denomination can locate the ethnic pastors and church workers who will help your vision become a reality. If your denomination has no developing plans for an ethnic church in your area but is willing to begin to move toward such a goal, have the patience to work with them. A project begun too quickly with too little forethought and too little financial support will likely fail, and it will be very difficult to get any support to try again. **Planning, financing, and beginning an ethnic ministry takes time!**

If your denomination is willing to work with you to develop a sharing relationship with an ethnic church, then you can move on toward mobilizing your congregation. If not, then you should either shelve the idea or look for other ways to bring it into being. Only when there is a reasonable expectation that a sharing relationship with an ethnic church can be developed should you begin mobilizing your congregation.

5.   Share your vision with the total congregation through every means at your disposal. (Again, this assumes that you have secured denominational backing for this project or have

made other arrangements which have a high probability of success.)
Use the pulpit, adult Bible studies, congregational meetings, articles
in your church newsletter, letters to your members, posters, and
any other creative way you can think of. Every method you use
should ooze with Great Commission vision and zeal. This will help
your entire congregation lay a Great Commission foundation in
their hearts and minds for this project and will help reinforce the
Great Commission foundation which you have already laid for your
leaders. Along with the spiritual motivation for this project, you
should also be providing accurate and specific information to your
congregation concerning what is involved in sharing mission,
ministry, and facilities with a congregation from another culture.
You also need to let your congregation know repeatedly that they
will soon be asked to make a decision on this matter. Do a
thorough job of informing your people. No one should think that
you tried to sneak this by them.

      6.   If you have not developed a core group of ethnics,
bring a representative of the culture with which you wish to move
into ministry into contact with your congregation for the purpose of
providing personal contact with and accurate information about that
culture. Choose this person carefully! It must be someone who has
accurate information about his/her culture and is able to
communicate effectively with your people. If your denomination has
an ethnic ministry specialist, he could help you find this person and
structure these congregational events. A good time for these
meetings would be on Sunday morning during the Sunday school
hour. Allow several weeks for this, as there will be much to share
and people will need time to absorb it all. If you have developed a
core group of this new ethnic community within your congregation,
they can effectively inform your congregation about their culture
and help to sensitize your people to them as human beings and
fellow members of the Body of Christ. Actually, this process of
informing and sensitizing your people to this new culture should
have begun when the core group began.

      7.   Your congregation will probably express four
different reactions to sharing mission, ministry, and facilities with
a church from a different culture. There will be a small group
which will zealously support the idea from the beginning. There

will be a large group which will support the idea but will have certain reservations. There will be another large group which will have many questions which they will want answered before they support the idea—these people will make sure you've done your homework. And there will be a small group which will be adamantly opposed to the idea, and nothing short of a personal appearance by God Himself could change their minds!

The first group will need no convincing; the second group will support the idea if you deal intelligently and honestly with their reservations; most of the third group will approve when their questions are answered; and many of those in the fourth group will end up finding a different church.

When people express opposition, meet with them privately and try to enlist their support—or at least their silence. Meeting privately with people who express major opposition can be time consuming but well worth your while in the long run. As you meet privately with people who have expressed opposition, don't make the meetings a test of your will against theirs. Try to find someone in your congregation who, in the beginning, had some major questions and reservations about entering into a sharing relationship with a group from a different culture but now supports the project for solid scriptural reasons. Take this person along as a resource. As this person shares his/her former opposition and present support for this project, she/he may well be your key to winning additional support for it. Another good idea is to form a prayer group to pray for you and those who express opposition as you seek to unite the congregation in this matter. This group should include people who've supported the idea from the beginning, those who formerly opposed the project but now support it, and even some of those who still have questions about it but will honestly seek the Lord's will in this matter. The group should also include members of the ethnic group with which you hope to enter into a sharing relationship.

8.   Ask for congregational authority to make arrangements to begin this sharing relationship. A special congregational meeting should be called for this one issue. Begin the meeting with a prayer which lays this decision before God and asks for His guidance for all in attendance and for the entire

congregation. Then have a Bible study with a Great Commission theme. Following the Bible study, review the mission, ministry, and stewardship of facilities statement. Give appropriate demographic information to justify the need for this sharing relationship. Tell the congregation how the project will be staffed and financed. Assure them that a Shared Ministries Committee composed of your members and members from the ethnic core group or ethnic church (or the ethnic pastor, if this is the beginning of a new ministry) will work out the details of the sharing relationship, and those details will be submitted to the congregation for approval. Give the approximate date the ministry is scheduled to begin if it is given approval. Someone who supports the concept should move to approve the idea. The motion should include the creation of the special committee to work out the details of the sharing relationship. (If, in your church polity, a group other than the congregation is the source of decision-making authority, proceed through this step with that group.)

Adequate time should be given for discussion, and then a vote should be taken. If approval is given, you are ready to move toward structuring the shape of this sharing relationship. At this point, the congregation, the denomination, and the ethnic pastor and/or the ethnic core group will cooperate to bring the idea to reality.

Having progressed this far, it would be well to stop and give thanks. Privately, in your prayers and personal devotions, thank God for having brought the project this far and for the people who have helped you. Publicly, in worship services and church meetings, thank God for His grace in this matter and for the many people who have caught the vision of sharing mission, ministry, and facilities with a congregation from another culture. Individually, thank people who have been of special help to you up to this point. You've said "please" many times already. Now it's time for some well-deserved "thank you's."

Appendix C
. . . GO!

(Implementation)

When the congregation approved the concept of sharing mission, ministry, and facilities with another cultural group, it should also have created a Committee on Shared Ministries which included representatives of both the host and guest congregations, along with an advisor from the denomination. The purpose of this committee is to work out the theological, programatic, and practical details of this sharing relationship. If the guest congregation will begin as a new mission at your church, the pastor called to begin the new church will probably be the only representative of the guest church. Also included as observer and advisor should be a representative of your denomination who has knowledge and experience in the field of shared ministries. He need not be at every meeting, but he should be included at the beginning, in the strategic meetings during the planning process, and at the final meetings as the covenant relationship which will give structure to the sharing relationship is finalized for presentation to the two congregations.

Sessions 1-4
The process begins with the committee joining together in prayer, fellowship and Bible study for four sessions. These Bible studies are included on separate sheets in the back of this book (pages 206-213).

Session 5
After the committee has spent four weeks sharing, praying, and studying the Bible together, it is ready to begin work on the shape of the sharing relationship. The purpose of this meeting (or meetings, if more than one is required) is to write the preamble or introduction to the covenant for shared ministry. The preamble summarizes the spiritual, congregational, and community basis for

168

sharing mission, ministry, and facilities. At this time, it would be useful to have the statement on the mission of the church, the concept of ministry, and the stewardship of facilities which was earlier worked out by the Church Council or Board of Directors. The preamble should be brief enough to be read as part of a special liturgy developed to celebrate the sharing relationship in a public worship service.

Open and close all meetings with prayer in both languages.

Before the closing prayer, sing at least one song which can be sung in both languages.

Give each person an opportunity to share briefly how their life has been or could be enriched by sharing mission, ministry, and facilities with another congregation.

Reflect on insights gained through the four weeks of Bible study.

It is important throughout this section that the relationship between the host and guest congregations never descends to the level of tenant-landlord and that you do your best to eliminate racism and paternalism from the sharing relationship which you establish.

Bruce McSpadden, in his book, *Manual on Shared Facilities*, has a section entitled "The Rights and Expectations of Congregations Sharing Facilities." Before anything else is done in the process of structuring the sharing relationship, the entire committee should read and discuss the ideas contained in that section. It is quoted here in its entirety.

A. The Rights of a Guest Congregation
A congregation worshiping in the building of another congregation has the right to expect at least the following:
1. *To be treated with dignity and respect as children of God.*
2. *The recognition and affirmation that they are a part of the Body of Christ and are carrying on the ministry of Christ.*
3. *The expectation that a church building is a tool for the ministry of the Body of Christ and is not a private possession of any particular individual or group.*

4.   *The right to adequate space and time to meet the needs of
their congregation, and a voice in the negotiation of such,
including kitchen facilities and pastoral office space.*

5.   *Participation in the negotiation of financial arrangements
between the congregations.*

6.   *The freedom to operate their own congregation without
interference within the terms of the agreement between the
congregations.*

7.   *The right to an exterior sign in their own language, large
enough to be visible from a distance and appropriate to the
decor of the building.*

8.   *That the building be kept clean and reasonably maintained.*

9.   *At least a three month's notice of the termination of the
agreement.*

10.   *The freedom to use decor, paraments and decorations for
their activities in keeping with their own cultural needs, as
they see fit.*

11.   *That all children be adequately supervised.*

12.   *That all commitments be honored as agreed upon, including
time and financial commitments.*

13.   *That property of particular individuals and/or groups be
honored and protected.*

14.   *The right to self-determination and the right to a voice in
the vital decisions that affect the life of their congregation.*

B. The Rights of a Host Congregation
*A congregation sharing its building with another congregation has
the right to expect at least the following:*

1.   *To be treated with dignity and respect as children of God.*

2.   *The recognition and affirmation that they are a part of the
Body of Christ and are carrying on the ministry of Christ.*

3.   *The expectation that a church building is a tool for the
ministry of the Body of Christ and is not a private
possession of any particular individual or group.*

4.   *That the building be kept clean and reasonably maintained.*

5.   *That the building be properly secured and that all utilities
be used appropriately and turned off when not in use.*

6.   *At least a three month's notice of the termination of the*

agreement.

7.   *That all children be adequately supervised.*

8.   *That all commitments be honored as agreed upon, including time and financial commitments.*

9.   *That property of particular individuals and/or groups be honored and protected.*

10.   *Adequate financial contributions from the guest congregation to cover its expenses and to share in the overall maintenance of the building. Amount to be mutually agreed upon.*

11.   *That members of the guest congregation will assist in the upkeep and maintenance of the building as appropriate and will assume a sense of responsibility for the overall care of the building.*

Make three lists on newsprint or chalkboards. The lists should bear the following headings:

1.   Spiritual basis for sharing
2.   Congregational basis for sharing
3.   Community basis for sharing

1.   *Spiritual basis for sharing.* This section might include the following: A section on the Great Commission as the basic purpose of the Christian church. A section on the uniqueness of the individual and the unity of all in the church as the Body of Christ. A section summarizing the mission statements of each church. A section which includes a joint mission statement by the two congregations. A section affirming the language and culture of both congregations and the importance of this sharing relationship as a witness to the community.

2.   *Congregational basis for sharing.* This section might include the following: A section on how the ministries of both congregations will be enhanced by this sharing relationship. A section affirming all church facilities as a trust from God to be used in His service, not a private possession for the exclusive use of one group. A section on how people in both congregations will be enriched because of the cultural sharing which will be a part of this relationship.

3.   *Community basis for sharing.* This section might include the following: A section summarizing demographic data from the community showing the need for ministering to the new culture. A section affirming the Great Commission's call to reach the world on our doorstep. A section affirming the need for this sharing relationship as a witness to the community of the unity possible within the Christian community.

After the committee puts all the suggestions on the newsprint or chalkboard, it needs to decide which ideas need to be included in the preamble.

Divide into three groups and assign each group the task of writing the first draft of one of the three sections.

Bring the committee back together and have each group read the draft it prepared. The whole committee then discusses the wording of each draft.

Spend time in prayer and reflection. Is this statement really what you want to say to the two congregations and to the world? Does this preamble lay adequate groundwork for sharing mission, ministry, and facilities? Is it clear enough to be understood if it is read as part of a worship service? Is there anything here which might be a problem for either congregation?

Assign a small group to refine and polish the statement for presentation at the next meeting. This group should be composed of two or four people with equal representation from both congregations.

Session 6

The purpose of these meetings is to formulate the principles which will be followed as both congregations develop their programs and as they negotiate time/space allocations. Time/space allocations relate to how the two congregations share the space available in the church facilities. These guiding principles will then become part of the covenant under the heading "Program Development and Time/Space Allocations."

Open and close all meetings with prayer in both languages.

Before the closing prayer, sing a song which can be sung in both languages.

The first order of business is to review and adopt the Preamble of the covenant. If changes need to be made, refer it back to the group chosen at the last meeting and ask them to make the needed changes.

Before beginning your work on this section of the covenant, you need to know the details of the sharing relationship which will be controlled by these principles. The "Program Development and Time/Space Allocation" section of the covenant covers a wealth of details, and you will want the guiding principles you establish to be broad enough and detailed enough to cover all the many possible questions which will arise in this area. Dr. Ralph F. Wilson ("How to Share Your Building Without Losing Your Church," *Ministries Today*, September-October 1987, pp. 52-53), lists specific points to be covered in a written agreement between host and guest congregations. Some are applicable in this section, and others will apply later in the writing of the covenant. His list follows.

A written agreement ought to consider the following points:
1. *The name of the guest church or group, and the name, address and telephone number of the pastor and another leader.*
2. *The dates for which the agreement is effective.*
3. *An initial list of rooms to be used and times of use, which may be changed by mutual agreement.*
4. *What kitchen, coffee pots, pans and table service may be used? Audio-visual equipment?*
5. *The procedure for scheduling special meetings.*
6. *Where to park and where not to park.*
7. *Cleaning arrangements. How much is expected of the guest group? Of the church custodian? Responsibilities for setting up, moving and putting away chairs and tables. Kitchen use and clean-up.*
8. *A statement that children must be supervised at all times.*
9. *Use of telephone, office space and storage space allotted to the guest congregation.*

10.   *Who will be responsible for keys and lock-up after each use? Is there a policy about duplication of keys?*
11.   *Signs identifying the guest congregation. How large and where?*
12.   *Request for participation in workdays to maintain the property.*
13.   *Financial responsibility for damages.*
14.   *For a separate congregation, a statement that the guest group's insurance should list the host church as "additional insured."*
15.   *The amount of shared use fee to be charged, if any, and when it is due.*
16.   *A procedure to terminate the relationship, if that becomes necessary. Try to provide enough notice so the guest congregation has time to locate other facilities, perhaps 60 to 90 days.*

Establish guidelines for negotiating time/space questions. These guidelines will help the two congregations utilize the facilities in ways which maximize their ministries and minimize friction between them. There are at least four possible ways for resolving time/space questions.

1.   The host church has priority in all time/space questions.
2.   The guest church has priority in all time/space questions.
3.   Time/space allocations are set on a "first come, first served" basis.
4.   Each time/space question is negotiated individually, taking into consideration its unique aspects.

There may be other ways which apply best in a given situation. The important thing to remember is that the principles established should be culturally appropriate for both congregations. Guidelines which sound very proper for an Anglo might be quite inappropriate for a Hispanic. The guidelines should be as nearly as possible equally workable for both groups. Neither should have a built-in cultural advantage based on the decisions made.

Establish a master calendar and guidelines for its use. These guidelines should be consistent with the guidelines for negotiating time/space allocations.

Discuss and adopt policies on facility use. A good outline for this discussion would be numbers 3, 4, 6, 7, 8, 9, 10, 11, 12, 13 and 14 of Dr. Wilson's checklist.

Establish guidelines for planning and financing joint activities, projects and ministries.

Establish guidelines for each congregation as it plans new programs and ministries which will require time/space allocations. Each congregation needs to know the future time/space needs which will be generated by the planned programs and ministries of both congregations. This allows for adequate time to plan for future demands on the facilities. Also, if there is good communication here, the two congregations may find ways to sponsor jointly certain programs and ministries.

A word of caution here. It takes time for two congregations to know each other well enough to plan much in the way of jointly sponsored programs and ministries. Any plans made at this point should be modest in scale. Joint worship services and social events may be the best way to begin.

If necessary, draft a statement which recommends renovations and/or new construction to make the facilities satisfactory for long-term shared ministry (if long-term sharing is the goal of the relationship). If significant renovation and/or new construction is deemed necessary, this would be a good time to recommend that a special committee be formed to look into precisely what is needed, when it will be needed and how it will be financed.

Assign a group of two or four people, with equal representation from both congregations, to write the proposed draft of the "Program Development and Time/Space Allocation" section of the covenant. This draft will be reviewed at the next meeting.

Hand out the worksheets for next meeting. The next meeting will begin negotiating agreements which will allow both congregations adequate time and space for their various ministries. To make that meeting fruitful, data on current and planned activities for both congregations need to be gathered. Worksheets for each major area of ministry need to be prepared.

One good way to do this is to have a worksheet for each church board or organization. A committee member can then meet with the board or organization assigned to him/her and work out the details of time and space requirements for the ministry of that board or organization. A suggested format for the worksheets is included in the back of the book (Worksheet I). You may make copies of this sheet.

Make sure there are plenty of these forms to cover every activity currently happening or planned. You don't want to leave anything out.

Divide the various areas of the ministry of each church among the appropriate committee members and ask them to come to the next meeting with an accounting of all space/time requirements of the areas of ministry assigned to them. It's critical that this be done thoroughly so that the next meeting can concentrate on how the two congregations can utilize the facilities in ways which are beneficial to all.

Session 7

The purpose of this session is to negotiate agreements which will allow both congregations adequate time and space for their various ministries. The items to be discussed and resolved under this heading may need several meetings to be covered. Spend as many meetings as necessary to cover completely all the areas of concern which are included here.

Open and close all meetings with prayer in both languages.

Before the closing prayer, sing at least one song which can be sung in both languages.

Review the final draft of the "Program Development and Time/Space Allocation" section and, if it's satisfactory, approve it as part of the covenant between the two congregations. If it isn't satisfactory, refer it back to the sub-committee with recommendations and have them return to the next meeting with another draft.

Introduce the purpose for the meetings. It is to begin to work out the details which will allow the principles contained in the "Program Development and Time/Space Allocation" section to work in the day-to-day ministries of each congregation. These meetings will work out the details of the time/space requirements for the present and planned ministries of each congregation and consider ideas for areas of ministry which can be jointly sponsored by both congregations.

Have a complete map of the church facilities prepared so that it can be referred to during the course of the meetings.

Have the host congregation and guest congregation members meet separately to draw up a complete time/space chart of their respective church's activities. A suggested format for this is included in the back of the book (Worksheet II).

Make four sets of weekly charts so you can see how the ministries of each church will utilize the facilities over the course of a month.

Make a second chart for each congregation which covers a full year. On this chart, show activities which occur less frequently than once a month. These less frequent activities need to fit into the monthly pattern of planned use. Perhaps the regular activities will have to be altered in a given month to accommodate one or more of these less frequent activities. Special concern will have to be devoted to the holiday seasons so that all of the special activities can run smoothly and to the satisfaction of all involved.

After the two groups have completed their charts, they should meet together again and share their charts with each other. Each group should fully explain all activities so all committee members understand the complete programs of both congregations. Any charted activities which represent planned rather than current programs should be clearly identified so the group understands both current needs and future plans of both congregations.

First, consider present activities. Are there any time/space conflicts? If so, the two congregations need to negotiate to eliminate the conflicts. The Program Development and Time/Space Allocation section of the covenant provides the guidelines for these negotiations. If the guidelines do not allow for negotiations which are satisfactory, they should be reviewed and changed. The Program Development and Time/Space Allocation section is supposed to be the section which allows for a positive resolution of time/space conflicts. At this point, you will begin to discover how well you wrote that section. This is where a map of all church facilities will be especially helpful. During negotiations, each church may need to accept an alternate time or space for an activity in order to resolve a conflict.

Second, consider planned activities. Do the future plans for facility use contain any possible conflicts? If so, this is the time to begin to negotiate to avoid these conflicts. Another point to consider at this time: Is is possible to make any of the future plans of either congregation into programs or ministries jointly sponsored by the two congregations?

If the two congregations plan any jointly sponsored programs or ministries, the practical steps toward such activities need to be outlined at this time. The "Program Development and Time/Space Allocation" section contains the guidelines for this kind of planning.

When you finish this section and before you begin the next, you need to have information gathered concerning current and future income and expenditures of both congregations. At least one representative from each congregation needs to gather the following information: budget, income, pledges (if pledges have been made) and per capita giving for the current year and, if possible, for the two previous years; projected budget needs for the next year; a breakdown of the cost of the operation and maintenance, repair, renovation and new construction costs; all insurance information; any other information which will have a financial impact on either congregation.

Session 8

The purpose of this meeting or meetings is to negotiate financial arrangements between the two congregations.

Open and close meetings with prayer in both languages.

Before closing, sing a song which can be sung in both languages.

Review the proposed draft of the section of the covenant titled "Program Development and Time/Space Allocations." If it is satisfactory, adopt it as part of the covenant. If not, give additional direction to the group doing the writing and ask them to submit another draft at the next meeting.

Remind all those in attendance that discussion of financial

arrangements grow out of our desire to share mission and ministry together. The relationship between the two congregations is not tenant/landlord, but "partner churches" fulfilling the Great Commission in our area. Rent will not be paid. Decisions will be made on how to share the costs of maintaining the church facilities in a way which is fair to both congregations and helps both congregations see the facilities as a gift from God and a tool for ministry.

Review the budget and giving patterns of each congregation.

Discuss those portions of the host church budget which deal with maintenance of facilities.

Review the usage patterns for the facilities which were detailed in the previous section.

Compare the worship attendance of the two congregations.

Decide on a formula for arriving at a fair share of facility costs to be assumed by each congregation. There are several ways of doing this. It can be very informal, with the guest church agreeing to pay a certain amount each year, quarter or month as a fair estimate of their fair share, based on their size and amount of facility usage. The denomination might suggest an amount which could be agreed to by both groups. You might want a very formal procedure for sharing the costs. This could be done by measuring the square footage of every room in your facility. Having done that, you could decide on a fair sharing relationship between the two congregations in two different ways.

First, you could develop a formula which considered three variables on all facility usage: square footage used, number of people using the square footage, and length of each use. The cost to each congregation for facility usage would be established based on these three factors. It would take a while to fine-tune such a formula, but once in place it can assure a sharing of costs based on actual use of the facility by both congregations.

Second, you could do a complete assessment of facility usage by each congregation and come up with a percentage of use by each congregation. For example, you might discover that the host congregation is responsible for 70 percent of facility usage and the guest congregation is responsible for 30 percent. Then take the total amount needed for facility maintenance and divide it according to the percentage of usage by each congregation. The example cited would mean that the host congregation would pay 70 percent of the facility maintenance budget and the guest congregation would pay 30 percent. However you decide to handle this issue, it should be made clear that the two congregations are sharing costs. One congregation is not charging rent to the other.

Decide on a formula for sharing the costs of facility maintenance and establish a process for annual review of the financial arrangements between the two congregations.

Discuss if there are other areas outside of facility maintenance where each congregation should share in the financial responsibility. Will there be shared office expenses or shared advertising expenses? If the two congregations will jointly sponsor an activity, program or ministry, they need to share in the expenses involved. Are there any other areas where expenses should be shared?

Discuss the insurance responsibilities of each congregation.

Once the committee has worked out an agreement on the sharing of financial responsibility, this agreement should be written down. A team of two or four people—with equal representation from both groups—should be assigned to bring a written draft of this section to the next meeting.

Session 9

The purpose of this session is to develop a permanent organizational structure to manage the sharing relationship between the two congregations, establish a procedure for periodic evaluation of the relationship and determine what procedures should be followed should a termination of the relationship become necessary. Again, this may take several meetings.

Open and close meetings with prayer in both languages.

Before the closing prayer, sing a song which can be sung in both languages.

Permanent organizational structures. First, decide on the type of relationship to be created between the two congregations. Is this to be a short-term sharing relationship to be terminated when the guest congregation has the finances to purchase property of its own? Is this to be a long-term sharing relationship with both congregations seeing their future together in the same facilities? Is this to be a relationship where the two congregations are separately incorporated, or should there be one umbrella corporate structure which covers both congregations? The ongoing relationship and future expectations of the two congregations need to be clearly stated.

Second, decide what kind of ongoing organizational structure is needed in order to deal properly with time/space allocations, financial arrangements, joint ministry planning and problem resolution. This will probably mean establishing some sort of permanent Shared Ministry Committee or Shared Ministry Board. This group, with equal representation from both congregations, will manage the ongoing relationships between the congregations and, where necessary, will ask both congregations to approve its actions. If the two congregations are to be parts of one corporate structure, a special committee needs to be formed to work out the details of that structure.

Evaluation. There should be at least one annual review of the sharing relationship between the two congregations. The committee could consider several options. The evalutation could be done at a joint meeting of the Church Councils or Boards of Directors of the two congregations. It could also be done at a joint meeting of the two congregations. The permanent Shared Ministry Committee or Board, in a meeting with additional representatives of each congregation and a district representative, could handle this evaluation. Some manageable method of annual review needs to be established so the sharing relationship can be fine-tuned on a regular basis and so the two churches can celebrate their ongoing life together. The annual evaluation can become a time of celebration of the relationship.

The committee needs to establish procedures for making changes in the covenant which is being submitted for approval to the two congregations. As time goes by, changes may need to be made, and now is the time to plan a way for those changes to be written into the agreement.

Termination of the relationship. Decide on the process that will be followed if the sharing relationship is to be terminated. This process must give the guest congregation a reasonable amount of time (at least 90 days is suggested) to find new facilities. The process should include an overall evaluation of the sharing relationship and should involve at least one representative from district.

Assign a group of two or four people, with equal representation from both congregations, to write a proposed draft of the section of the covenant dealing with organizational structures, evaluation and termination. They are to present their draft to the appropriate person or persons before the meeting which finalizes the covenant.

Session 10

Finalizing, ratifying and celebrating. The purpose of this section is to finalize the written covenant, have each congregation ratify it, and celebrate the beginning of the covenant relationship between the two congregations.

Open and close meetings with prayer in both languages.

Before the closing prayer, sing a song which can be sung in both languages.

Once the final section of the proposed covenant has been completed, it should be given to the committee chairperson, who then puts it together with the other sections and mails copies of the completed covenant to all members of the committee, at least one week prior to the next meeting. At that meeting, the entire covenant is discussed, a section at a time. If sections are not satisfactory, they can be reworked by the comittee or assigned to a small group within the committee. This final evaluation of the covenant may be done in one meeting or may take several meetings. Make sure adequate time is spent on this process. Once the committee is satisfied with the covenant, it should approve it and recommend it to both congregations. The congregations, using whatever is the appropriate method for them, should discuss the covenant and either ratify it or send it back to the committee for revisions. Once the covenant is ratified by both congregations, it becomes the official description of the sharing relationship between the two groups.

Once both congregations have ratified the covenant, a joint, bilingual worship service should be planned to celebrate the covenant and the sharing relationship to which both congregations are committing themselves.

Appendix D
SHARING FACILITIES WITH AN ETHNIC CHURCH OF A DIFFERENT DENOMINATION

If your church is in a culturally mixed area, you may not wish to extend yourself to enter into a sharing relationship with an ethnic church of your denomination, but that doesn't mean you will not face this challenge. In most culturally mixed areas, there are religious groups actively looking for facilities. Sooner or later, they will probably contact you. If this happens, how should you proceed?

If the challenge to enter a sharing relationship comes to you, much of the section "The pastor prepares himself for ethnic ministry" is not applicable. You will need to adapt the section "Preparing the congregation," but most of it will be needed even if the group you will be working with is not from your denomination. You will also need to do some adaptation of the section "Implementation." It is important to note that even though you are not dealing with an ethnic congregation of your own denomination, this does not mean that the input of your regional denominational representatives can be left out.

First, you need to find out if your denomination has plans for ethnic ministry in your area. If so, would your sharing relationship with this congregation of a different denomination harm those plans? Perhaps your denomination was planning on your facilities being available for use by them in developing an ethnic congregation. Second, perhaps your denomination can give you additional information on items to consider when you tell them which denomination you intend to work with in this sharing relationship. Third, the reason the group which contacted you may be in need of a facility is that they have been unable to work well in other sharing relationships. Your denomination may be acquainted with this group and could give you some information you would want to consider before you begin any sharing relationship. The general thought here is that it is preferable for you to enter into a sharing relationship with a congregation of your own denomination if you feel led to share your facilities.

Regardless of whether you enter a sharing relationship with an ethnic congregation from your own or another denomination, you will need a written covenant which will structure that relationship. Without a written covenant, the sharing relationship can be destroyed when there is a change of leadership in either congregation. With a written covenant, the sharing relationship can continue to flourish even when there are major leadership changes in either congregation. Also, if things are not written down, the chances of misunderstandings and conflicts between the two congregations are enormously magnified.

The Roles of Host and Guest Pastors

Bruce McSpadden, in his excellent resource titled *Manual on Shared Facilities*, has a section titled "Pastoral Leadership." It gives solid advice on the kind of relationship needed between the host and guest pastors.

A major factor in the success or failure of a shared facility relationship is the pastoral leadership of both congregations and the relationship between the two pastors.

A.   The Host Pastor

The pastor of the host congregation must see the sharing of its building with another congregation as a significant aspect of ministry that can benefit the host congregation as well as the new congregation. Such a commitment involves a willingness to spend time, effort, and emotional energy in seeing that it works, in coordinating it, resolving conflicts, in utilizing it for creative change within her/his congregation. If the host pastor is not in full support of this ministry, it will not work.

There are two critically important roles for the host pastor of a successful venture in a shared facility. First, he is to be the interpreter of the ministry as one who sees this as an opportunity to be the Body of Christ and puts it in a theological context of mission and ministry to his/her congregation, to the ethnic constituency and to the community. This also involves taking the leadership in developing a mission design. Second, he is to be the overall coordinator, liaison, and buffer between the two congregations. This involves protecting the guest congregation from unhelpful complaining and conflict. Nothing makes a guest congregation feel more unwanted than to hear constant complaining from members of the host congregation. It is important for the host pastor to be visible to the guest congregation.

B.   *The Guest Pastor*
       The guest pastor needs to have a vision of cooperative ministry and be able to interpret to members of the guest congregation that they are not tenants in someone's building, but they are part of the body of Christ in the Lord's building. The pastor plays a key role as liaison and interpreter between the two congregations, working closely with the host pastor. It is important for the guest pastor to be visible to the host congregation. If such a relationship is to be truly a cooperative ministry, then the guest pastor needs to be willing to share with the host pastor where racism and paternalism are experienced. This may be very difficult, since it can be done only in a context of acceptance and trust. Both pastors need to have a vision of sharing that goes beyond mere expediency to a shared ministry that enables a covenantal relationship.

C.   *Relationship Between the Two Pastors*
       A team relationship is needed between the two pastors. There should be regular meetings with opportunity for sharing, for dealing with specific issues, and for developing plans for cooperative ministry. If there is a language barrier, a key lay person may be part of the team to interpret. There must be a sense of trust and confidence between the pastors.
       A few additional observations might be added to this. It is important that there be a warm personal friendship between the host and guest pastors. A friendship which expresses itself in shared meals between the two pastors, opportunities for the host and guest pastors and their families to get together for food and fellowship and shared prayer between the host and guest pastors can be very

beneficial. As a close friendship develops between the host and guest pastors, a basis for resolving any future conflicts between the two congregations is being built. In the final analysis, however, this friendship is not for business purposes. It is developed for the joy of experiencing close fellowship with the beautiful people God has brought into your life.

There should be enough mutual respect that neither pastor interferes in the internal affairs of the other congregation. Each pastor should use every opportunity to affirm the integrity, autonomy and uniqueness of both congregations.

Appendix E
CHECKLISTS, BIBLE STUDIES, AND WORKSHEETS

Checklist for Appendix A
GET READY . . .

MOVING TOWARD MINISTRY WITH ANOTHER CULTURAL GROUP
(The Host Pastor)

The host pastor prepares himself for ethnic ministry:

1. Prayer
2. Congregational analysis
3. Community analysis
4. Get to know representatives of major ethnic groups in your area
5. Keep up with news from ethnic communities
6. Decide with which ethnic group you want to enter into a partnership ministry
7. Find areas where your congregation can serve the ethnic group with which you want to enter a partnership ministry
8. Read books on the culture and history of the group with which you want to enter into a partnership ministry
9. Become a little familiar with their language
10. Form a core group within your congregation of the ethnics with whom you wish to minister

Checklist for Appendix B
. . . GET SET . . .

MOVING TOWARD MINISTRY WITH ANOTHER CULTURAL GROUP
(The Host Pastor and his Congregation)

1. Ask for God's direction
2. Share your vision of sharing mission, ministry and facilities with a church from another culture with a small group in your congregation
3. Share your vision with your congregational leaders
4. Contact your denomination
5. Share your vision with your total congregation
6. Bring a representative of the culture with which you wish to enter into ministry into contact with your congregation
7. Handle opposition
8. Get congregational authority to begin

Checklist for Appendix C
. . . GO!

IMPLEMENTING A SHARING OF MISSION, MINISTRY AND FACILITIES
(The Host Congregation and its Pastor, the Guest Congregation and its pastor, and the Denomination in Partnership)

1. Form a Committee on Shared Ministries
2. Hold four Bible studies with the committee
3. Write the preamble of the covenant which will join the two congregations in ministry
4. Write the program development and time/space allocation sections of the covenant
5. Negotiate time/space allocations for the two congregations
6. Write the financial arrangements section of the covenant
7. Write the sections of the covenant which deal with permanent organizational structures to manage the sharing relationship, periodic evaluation of the relationship, and termination
8. Finalize, ratify and celebrate the covenant

MOVING TOWARD MINISTRY WITH ANOTHER CULTURAL GROUP

A checklist for the pastor before he begins exploring the possibilities of leading his congregation into a partnership ministry with an ethnic congregation

1. What spiritual gifts do you have which will help you be successful in leading your church into partnership with an ethnic congregation?
2. What drawbacks do you have which will be a problem for you?
3. What prejudices do you have concerning the group you want to work with?
4. How much opposition to this idea do you expect from members of your congregation?
5. With how much opposition are you willing to deal?
6. Where is opposition likely to come from and how will you handle it?
7. What are your reasons for wanting to be involved in ethnic ministry?
8. How does ethnic ministry fit into your understanding of the mission of the Church?
9. How does ethnic ministry fit into your understanding of the stewardship of your facilities?

JOINT COMMITTEE—WEEK ONE
THE CHRISTIAN CHURCH'S FIRST CROSS-CULTURAL MINISTRY EFFORT

Open with prayer in both languages.

FELLOWSHIP
Give each person the opportunity to respond to the following sharing questions:
1.   Where were you living between the ages of 7 and 12, and what were the winters like?
2.   How did you heat your home during this time?
3.   What was the center of warmth in your life during this time? (This can be a place in the house, a time of year, or a person.)
4.   When did God become a "warm" person to you, and how did it happen?

BIBLE STUDY
Matthew 28:19-20—How does the Great Commission relate to our community, our congregations and our desire to share mission, ministry and facilities?

Acts 1:8—What is necessary before mission can begin, and what does that mean for us today?

What is our Jerusalem, Judea, Samaria and the ends of the earth?

Where do mission and ministry begin?

Acts 2:1-11, 41—What is the basis of successful cross-cultural ministry?

Why did the Holy Spirit make it possible for the disciples to communicate to the many ethnic groups gathered in Jerusalem in their own languages?

What can we learn from this in the areas of language and culture?

In verse 41, what were the results of this first venture into cross-cultural ministry?

How do you expect God to bless our ministries?

Sing at least one song which can be sung in both languages.

Close with prayer in both languages.

JOINT COMMITTEE—WEEK TWO
FROM PREJUDICE TO MISSION

Open with prayer in both languages.

FELLOWSHIP
Give each person the opportunity to respond to the following sharing questions:
1.   Where were you born and what was your home town like?
2.   If you could give the world one gift (outside of faith in Jesus) what would that gift be and why would you give it?
3.   Why are you a member of this committee?

BIBLE STUDY
Acts 10:1-23—Where is there evidence of hunger for the Gospel among those who will be touched by our sharing mission, ministry and facilities?

How did Peter reveal his prejudices in versees 9-16? What were they?

What prejudices do you have toward another ethnic group or the group you propose to work with? (Both groups should struggle with this.)

How have you experienced racial/ethnic barriers in the larger church and in your own congregation?

How have you experienced oneness in Christ across racial/ethnic barriers?

How did God deal with Peter's prejudice and how does that apply to us?

What was the result of Peter reaching out to Cornelius?

In what areas will it be difficult for our two congregations to bridge their cultural differences? How can these problems best be resolved?

What will happen if we enter into a loving sharing of mission, ministry and facilities?

Sing at least one song which can be sung in both languages.

Close with prayer in both languages.

JOINT COMMITTEE—WEEK THREE
OWNERSHIP OR STEWARDSHIP?

Open with prayer in both languages.

FELLOWSHIP
Give each person the opportunity to respond to the following sharing questions:
1.   If you had a million dollars, what would be the first thing you would buy?
2.   What is your most valued material possession? Why is it so valuable to you?
3.   If you woke up in the middle of the night and your house was burning down, what would you rescue from the fire before your house burned down? Why?

BIBLE STUDY
Psalm 24:1, 1 Kings 8:27, Joshua 5:13-15—Summarize the meaning of each passage. What does each tell us of God's relationship to the earth and our responsibilities as good stewards?

Matthew 25:14-30—Why was the master pleased with the servants who were given the five and the two talents?

What was the fatal sin of the servant who received the one talent?

How does this apply to our stewardship of facilities?

Luke 12:13-21—What was the fatal sin of the rich fool?

How does this apply to our stewardship of facilities?

Sing at least one song that can be sung in both languages.

Close with prayer in both languages.

JOINT COMMITTEE—WEEK FOUR
A VISION OF HEAVEN APPLIED TO EARTH

Open with prayer in both languages.

FELLOWSHIP
Give each person the opportunity to respond to the following sharing questions:

1. What do you think heaven will be like?
2. When you get to heaven, what is the first thing you want to do?

BIBLE STUDY
Revelation 7:9-12—Who are the people referred to in verse 9?

Have the people in heaven lost their uniqueness? Why or why not?

What unites everyone in heaven? See especially verses 10 and 12.

How can we experience a bit of this vision becoming reality through sharing mission, ministry and facilities?

How can our two congregations celebrate the unity of heaven through special shared events?

What is your dream or vision for your church?

Share some insights you have gained during these sessions. Are there ways to share what you have experienced with others in both congregations?

Sing at least one song which can be sung in both languages.

Close with prayer in both languages.

WORKSHEET I

Board or Organization Name _____

Activity#1_____

Activity is current   planned

Start-up date (if planned) _____

Frequencyofmeetings_____

Meeting days _____ Meeting times _____

Number of people involved per meeting _____

Amount and kind of space needed _____

Is there room for negotiation regarding meeting days, times and the kind of space preferred? _____

Activity#2_____

Activity is current   planned

Start-up date (if planned) _____

Frequencyofmeetings_____

Meeting days _____ Meeting times _____

Number of people involved per meeting _____

Amount and kind of space needed _____

Is there room for negotiation regarding meeting days, times and the kind of space preferred? _____

Activity#3 _____

Activity is current   planned

Start-up date (if planned) _____

Frequency of meetings _____

Meeting days _____ Meeting times _____

Number of people involved per meeting _____

Amount and kind of space needed _____

Is there room for negotiation regarding meeting days, times and the kind of space preferred? _____

WORKSHEET II

SUN MON TUES WED THURS FRI SAT

Act. #1 _____

Time_____

Space
Required_____

Act. #2 _____

Time_____

Space
Required_____

Act. #3 _____

Time_____

Space
Required_____

Act. #4 _____

Time_____

Space
Required_____

Act. #5 _____

Time_____

Space
Required_____

Act. #6 _____

Time_____

Space
Required_____

Act. #7 _____

Time_____

Space
Required_____

ENDNOTES

CHAPTER 1

1. Ronald Takaki, editor, *From different Shores*, (New York: Oxford University Press, 1987), 29.

2. Bernard A. Weisberger, *Many People, One Nation*, (Boston: Houghton Mifflin Co., 1987), 41.

3. Ibid., 40-41.

4. Ibid., 44.

5. Thomas Sowell, *Ethnic America*, Copyright 1981 by BasicBooks, Inc., a division of HarperCollins Publishers, Inc., New York. Page 47.

6. From *The Germans in America*, by Virginia Brainard Kunz. Copyright 1966 by Lerner Publications Company, Minneapolis, MN. Used with permission. Page 25.

7. Sowell, *Ethnic America*, 55.

8. Ibid., 68.

9. Weisberger, *Many People, One Nation*, 81.

10. Ibid., 80.

11. Sowell, *Ethnic America*, 196.

12. Weisberger, *Many People, One Nation*, 250.

13. Ibid., 251.

14. Sowell, *Ethnic America*, 209.

15. Ibid., 211.

16. Ibid., 224.

17. Ibid., 216.

18. Ibid., 77.

19. Charles Wollenberg, editor, *Ethnic Conflict in California History*, (Los Angeles: Tinnon Brown, Inc., 1970), 68.

20. Sowell, *Ethnic America*, 137.

21. E. Allen Richardson, *Strangers in This Land*, 94. Reprinted with permission of the Pilgrim Press, Cleveland, Ohio, 1988.

22. Wollenberg, *Ethnic Conflict in California History*, 73.

23. Ibid., 92.

24. Sowell, *Ethnic America*, 137.

25. Ibid., 137.

26. Weisberger, *Many People, One Nation*, 188.

27. David M. Reimers, *Still the Golden Door*, (Copyright 1985, Columbia University Press, New York), 4. Reprinted with the permission of the publisher.

28. Sowell, *Ethnic America*, 140.

29. Reimers, *Still the Golden Door*, 4.

30. Sowell, *Ethnic America*, 148.

31. Ibid., 23.

32. Weisberger, *Many People, One Nation*, 116.

33. Ibid., 117-118.

34. Sowell, *Ethnic America*, 21.

35. Ibid., 22.

36. Ibid., 22.

37. Ibid., 27.

38. Ibid., 160.

39. Ibid., 162.

40. Ibid., 163.

41. Reimers, *Still the Golden Door*, 5.

42. Sowell, *Ethnic America*, 167.

43. Ibid., 171.

44. Ibid., 172.

45. Ibid., 175.

46. Weisberger, *Many People, One Nation*, 281.

47. Richardson, *Strangers in This Land*, 79.

48. Reimers, *Still the Golden Door*, 7.

49. Sowell, *Ethnic America*, 255.

50. Reimers, *Still the Golden Door*, 215-216.

51. Sowell, *Ethnic America*, 255.

52. Reimers, *Still the Golden Door*, 130-131.

53. Ibid., 110-111.

54. Weisberger, *Many People, One Nation*, 311.

55. H. Brett Melendy, *Asians in America: Filipinos, Koreans and East Indians*, 37. Excerpted with permission of Twayne Publishers and the San Francisco Chronicle, an imprint of Macmillan Publishing Company, Copyright 1977 by G. K. Hall & Co,.

56. Ibid., 42.

57. Ibid., 42.

58. Ibid., 74.

59. Ibid., 69.

60. Ibid., 62.

61. Ibid., 66.

62. Sowell, *Ethnic America*, 228.

63. Ibid., 230.

64. Ibid., 231.

65. Ibid., 232.

66. Weisberger, *Many People, One Nation*, 291.

67. Ibid., 292.

68. Reimers, *Still the Golden Door*, 157.

69. Ibid., 157.

70. Ibid., 173.

71. Victor Alba, *The Latin Americans*, (Preiger Publishers, an imprint of Greenwood Publishing Group, Inc., Westport, CT, 1969), 5.

72. Ibid., 7.

73. Ibid., 7.

74. Simon Collier, Harold Blakemore and Thomas E. Skidmore, editors, *The Cambridge Encyclopedia of Latin America and the Caribbean*, (Cambridge: Cambridge University Press, 1985), 310-311. Used by permission.

75. Reimers, *Still the Golden Door*, 175.

76. Ibid., 175.

77. Weisberger, *Many People, One Nation*, 306.

78. Reimers, *Still the Golden Door*, 177.

79. Ibid., 178-179.

80. Ibid., 176-179.

81. Ibid., 181.

82. Richardson, *Strangers in This Land*, 23.

83. Alejandro Portes and Rubén G. Rumbaut, *Immigrant America: A Portrait*. Copyright © 1990 The Regents of the University of California. Page 21.

84. Richard Carlson and Bruce Goldman, *2020 Visions: Long View of a Changing World*, (Copyright 1991 by Richard Carlson, Bruce Goldman and the Stanford Alumni Association, Stanford, CA), 63.

85. Ibid., 62.

CHAPTER 2

1. Reprinted from *The Book of Concord*, by Theodore G. Tappert, copyright 1959 Fortress Press. Used by permission of Augsburg Fortress. Page 464.

2. Paul G. Hiebert, *Cultural Anthropology*, (Grand Rapids: Baker Book House, 1983), 25.

3. Ibid., 376.

4. Edward T. Hall, *Beyond Culture*, (Garden City, New York: Anchor Press/Doubleday, 1976), 43.

5. William Petersen, Michael Novak, Philip Gleason, *Concepts of Ethnicity*, (Cambridge: The Belknap Press of Harvard University Press, 1982), 29.

6. *Open Windows, Swinging Doors*, by Frank C. Laubach. Copyright 1955, Regal Books, Ventura, CA 93003. Used by permission. Pages 5-6.

7. I speak here as an Anglo reflecting Anglo-American culture.

8. Some people don't like what they call "hyphenated Americans," but when dealing with the new or persistent ethnic communities there seems to be no escaping it. In this example, it would be unfair to call the Anglo an American and the Vietnamese-American simply a Vietnamese, for he may already be a citizen of America or at least working toward that goal. Using hyphenated designations is not an attempt to make a statement about ethnicity. We are simply trying to be accurate, and for most of the new ethnic communities today hyphenated references are necessary for accuracy.

9. These terms come from Edward T. Hall's book, *Beyond Culture*.

10. These terms also come from *Beyond Culture*.

11. Hall, *Beyond Culture*, 17.

12. Ibid., 18-19.

13. Marvin K. Mayers, *Christianity Confronts Culture*, (Grand Rapids: Academie Books, Zondervan Publishing House, 1987), 159.

CHAPTER 3

1. Bernard A. Weisberger, *Many People, One Nation*, (Boston: Houghton Mifflin Company, 1987), 31.

2. E. Allen Richardson, *Strangers in This Land*, (Reprinted with permission of the Pilgrim Press, Cleveland, Ohio), 23.

3. Ibid., 109.

4. Ronald Takaki, editor, *From Different Shores*, (New York: Oxford University Press, 1987), 16.

5. Ibid., 15.

6. Richardson, *Strangers in This Land*, 60.

7. William Petersen, Michael Novak, and Philip Gleason, *Concepts of Ethnicity*, (Cambridge: The Belknap Press of Harvard University Press, 1982), 69.

8. Richardson, *Strangers in This Land*, 59.

9. Ibid., 61.

10. Richard A. Easterlin, David Ward, William S. Bernard, and Reed Ueda, *Immigration*, (Cambridge: The Belknap Press of Harvard University Press, 1982), 90.

11. Alejandro Portes and Rubén G. Rumbaut, *Immigrant America: A Portrait*. Copyright © 1990 The Regents of The University of California. Page 108.

12. Richardson, *Strangers in This Land*, 113.

13. Ibid., 113.

14. Petersen, Novak and Gleason, *Concepts of Ethnicity*, 90.

15. Weisberger, *Many People, One Nation*, 230.

16. Portes and Rumbaut, *Immigrant America*, 149.

17. Ibid., 185.

18. Ibid., 185-186.

19. Weisberger, *Many People, One Nation*, 215.

20. Ibid., 214 and 216.

21. Richardson, *Strangers in This Land*, 114.

22. Nathan Glazer, *Ethnic Dilemmas, 1964-1982*, (Cambridge: Harvard University Press, 1983), 103-104.

23. Petersen, Novak and Gleason, *Concepts of Ethnicity*, 123-124.

CHAPTER 4

1. Alejandro Portes and Rubén G. Rumbaut, *Immigrant America: A Portrait.* Copyright © 1990 The Regents of The University of California. Page 169.

2. Ibid., 141.

3. William Petersen, Michael Novak, Philip Gleason, *Concepts of Ethnicity*, (Cambridge: The Belknap Press of Harvard University Press, 1982), 121.

4. Will Herberg, *Protestant—Catholic—Jew*, (Garden City, New York: Anchor Books, Doubleday and Company, Inc., 1960).

5. Ronald Takaki, editor, *From Different Shores*, (New York: Oxford University Press, 1987), 23.

6. Win Arn, editor, *The Pastor's Church Growth Handbook, Vol. 1*, (Pasadena, California: Church Growth Press, 1979), 178.

7. Ibid, 179.

8. Consider the controversy raised by the book by David S. Luecke, *Evangelical Style and Lutheran Substance*, (St. Louis: Concordia Publishing House, 1988).

9. David W. Augsburger, *Pastoral Counseling Across Cultures*, (Philadelphia: The Westminster Press, 1986), 72. Used by permission.

10. Charles H. Kraft, *Christianity in Culture*, (Maryknoll, New York: Orbis Books, 1979), 93.

11. Ibid., 93.

12. William Petersen, Michael Novak, Philip Gleason, *Concepts of Ethnicity*, 51.

13. David W. Augsburger, *Pastoral Counseling Across Cultures*,
14. Donald McGavran, *The Clash Between Christianity and Cultures*, (Grand Rapids: Baker Book House, 1974).

15. Ibid., 38-39.

16. Ibid., 39-41.

17. Ibid., 46.

18. Ibid., 46.

19. Ibid., 47.

20. Ibid., 47.

21. Ibid., 47.

22. Ibid., 48.

23. Ibid., 48.

24. Ibid., 81.

25. William J. Larkin, Jr., *Culture and Biblical Hermeneutics*, (Grand Rapids: Baker Book House, 1988), 130.

26. David J. Hesselgrave and Edward Rommen, *Contextualization*, (Grand Rapids: Baker Book House, 1989), xi.

CHAPTER 5

1. Edward T. Hall, *Beyond Culture*, (Garden City, New York: Anchor Press/Doubleday, 1976), 155-156.

2. Ibid, 161.

3. David W. Augsburger, *Pastoral Counseling Across Cultures*, (Philadelphia: The Westminster Press, 1986), 183.

4. Ibid., 183.

5. Ibid., 29.

6. Ibid., 29-30.

7. Ibid., 30.

8. John Higham, *Send These to Me: Immigrants in Urban America,* (New York: Atheneum, 1984), 208.

9. Ronald Takaki, editor, *From Different Shores,* (New York: Oxford University Press, 1987), 23.

ACKNOWLEDGEMENTS

Alba, Victor. *The Latin Americans*. Westport, CT: Praeger Publishers, an imprint of Greenwood Publishing Group, Inc., 1969.

Arn, Dr. Win, ed. *The Pastor's Church Growth Handbook, Vol. 1.* Pasadena: Church Growth Press, 1979.

Augsburger, David W. *Pastoral Counseling Across Cultures.* Philadelphia: The Westminster Press, 1986.

Carlson, Richard and Bruce Goldman. *2020 Visions: Long View of a Changing World*. Stanford, California: Stanford Alumni Association, 1991.

Collier, Simon, Harold Blakemore and Thomas E. Skidemore, eds. *The Cambridge Encyclopedia of Latin America and the Caribbean.* Cambridge: Cambridge University Press, 1985.

Easterlin, Richard A., David Ward, William S. Bernard, and Reed Ueda. *Immigration.* Cambridge: The Belknap Press of Harvard University Press, 1982.

Glazer, Nathan. *Ethnic Dilemmas, 1964-1982.* Cambridge: Harvard University Press, 1983.

Hall, Edward T. *Beyond Culture.* Garden City, New York: Anchor Press/Doubleday, 1976.

Hesselgrave, David J. and Edward Rommen. *Contxtualization.* Grand Rapids: Baker Book House, 1989.

Hiebert, Paul G. *Cultural Anthropology.* Grand Rapids: Baker Book House, 1983.

Higham *Send These To Me: Immigrants in Urban America.* New York: Atheneum, 1984.

Kraft, Charles H. *Christianity in Culture.* Maryknoll, New York: Orbis Books, 1979.

Kunz, Virginia Brainard. *The Germans in America.* Minneapolis:

Lerner Publications Co., 1966.

Larkin, William J., Jr. *Culture and Biblical Hermeneutics*. Grand Rapids: Baker Book House, 1988.

Laubach, Frank C. *Open Windows, Swinging Doors*. Ventura, California: Regal Books Division, G/L Publications, 1955.

Mayers, Marvin K. *Christianity Confronts Culture*. Grand Rapids: Zondervan Publishing House, 1987.

McGavran, Donald. *The Clash Between Christianity and Cultures*. Washington, D.C.: Canon Press, 1974. Administered by Baker Book House, Grand Rapids, Michigan.

McSpadden, Bruce. *Manual on Shared Facilities*. New York: Global Ministries/United Methodist Church, 1986.

Melendy, H. Brett. *Asians in America: Filipinos, Koreans and East Indians*. Boston: Twayne Publishers, a division of G. K. Hall and Co., 1977.

Petersen, William, Michael Novak, Philip Gleason. *Concepts of Ethnicity*. Cambridge: The Belknap Press of Harvard University Press, 1982.

Portes, Alejandro and Rubén G. Rumbaut. *Immigrant America: A Portrait*. Berkeley: The Regents of University of California Press, 1990.

Reimers, David M. *Still the Golden Door*. New York: Columbia University Press, 1985.

Richardson, E. Allen. *Strangers in This Land*. New York: The Pilgrim Press, 1988.

Sowell, Thomas. *Ethnic America*. New York: BasicBooks, a division of HarperCollins Publishers, Inc., 1981.

Takaki, Ronald, ed. *From Different Shores*. New York: Oxford University Press, 1987.

Tappert, Theodore G. *The Book of Concord*. Philadelphia: Fortress Press/Augsberg Fortress, 1959.

Weisberger, Bernard A. *Many People, One Nation*. Boston:

Houghton Mifflin Company, 1987.

Wilson, Ralph F. *Ministries Today*. "How to Share Your Building Without Losing Your Church." Article, September-October, 1987.

FOR FURTHER STUDY

Baake, Ray. *The Urban Christian.* Downers Grove, IL: InterVarsity Press, 1987.

Claerbaut, David. *Urban Ministry.* Grand Rapids: Zondervan Publishing House, 1983.

Conn, Harvie M. *A Clarified Vision for Urban Mission.* Grand Rapids, Michigan: Zondervan Publishing House, 1987.

Filbeck, David. *Social Context and Proclamation.* Pasadena: William Carey Library, 1985.

Greenway, Roger S. and Timothy M. Monsma. *Cities: Mission's New Frontier.* Grand Rapids: Baker Book House, 1989.

Herberg, Will. *Protestant—Catholic—Jew.* Garden City, New York: Anchor Books, Doubleday And Company, Inc., 1960.

Hopler, Thom. *A World of Difference.* Downers Grove, Illinois: InterVarsity Press, 1981.

Luecke, David S. *Evangelical Style and Lutheran Substance.* St. Louis: Concordia Publishing House, 1988.

Lupton, Robert D. *Theirs is the Kingdom—Celebrating the Gospel in Urban America.* San Francisco: Harper and Row, 1989.

Mee, Charles L., Jr. *The Genius of the People.* New York: Harper and Row, 1987.

Niebuhr, H. Richard. *Christ and Culture.* New York: Harper and Brothers, 1951.

Wollenberg, Charles, ed. *Ethnic Conflict in California History.* Los Angeles: Tinnon Brown, Inc., 1970.

INDEX